Friendships Through the Life Course

Volume 161 Sage Library of Social Research

RECENT VOLUMES IN . . .
SAGE LIBRARY OF SOCIAL RESEARCH

Friendships Through the Life Course

Oral Biographies in Old Age

Sarah H. Matthews

Volume 161
SAGE LIBRARY OF
SOCIAL RESEARCH

SAGE PUBLICATIONS
The Publishers of Professional Social Science
Beverly Hills Newbury Park London New Delhi

For information address:

SAGE Publications, Inc.
275 South Beverly Drive
Beverly Hills, California 90212

SAGE Publications Inc.
2111 West Hillcrest Drive
Newbury Park
California 91320

SAGE Publications Ltd.
28 Banner Street
London EC1Y 8QE
England

SAGE PUBLICATIONS India Pvt. Ltd.
M-32 Market
Greater Kailash I
New Delhi 110 048 India

Printed in the United States of America

Library of Congress Cataloging-in-Publication Data

Matthews, Sarah H.
  Friendships through the life course.

  (Sage library of social research ; v. 161)
  Bibliography: p.
  1. Interpersonal relations. 2. Friendship—
Research. 3. Life cycle, Human. 4. Aged—United
States—Interviews. 5. Sociology—Biographical
method. I. Title. II. Series.
HM32.M366   1986   158′.25   85-27619
ISBN 0-8039-2641.3
ISBN 0-8039-2642-1 (pbk.)

FIRST PRINTING

CONTENTS

end of Matthews contents

For Jetse Sprey, with affection and esteem.

ACKNOWLEDGMENTS

This book would not have been possible without the help of many people. To the elders who shared their biographies, I owe the greatest debt. Each made a unique and remarkable contribution, and my greatest hope is that my use of their life stories is both faithful and valuable. Kenneth Gill contributed superb interviewing skills and shared his perceptive insights as the data were being collected and organized. The manuscript was read in whole, or in part, and encouraged on its way by Victor Marshall, Marjorie Main, and Corinne Nydegger. Without their support I might well have foundered. Barbara Hampton kept me on track with the word processor and helped type the manuscript. Blanche Young eliminated my "tortuous prose." Margaret Grier, while not contributing directly, provided more help than she knew. From beginning to end, Jetse Sprey contributed critical comments and fruitful suggestions. Without his advice and support, the book without doubt would be a lesser product. Any flaws, of course, are my own. The research was supported by Grant AG02251 from the National Institute on Aging.

Some of the material was published previously in "Analyzing Topical Oral Biographies of Old People: The Case of Friendship," *Research on Aging* 5:569-589 (1983), and "Friendship in Old Age: Biography and Circumstance," in Victor W. Marshall (ed.), *Later Life: The Social Psychology of Aging* (Beverly Hills, CA: Sage, 1986), and we are grateful for its use.

—S. H. M.

CHAPTER 1

FRIENDSHIPS IN
BIOGRAPHICAL CONTEXT

This book is about friendship within the context of people's lives. It is not, or at least not only, about current networks of social support but is about the reciprocal relationship between individuals' biographies—their pasts, presents, and futures—and those whom they identify as friends. My interest in this subject was sparked by old women, informants for earlier research (Matthews, 1979), who distinguished between the quality of their relationships with old and more recently acquired friends. One woman, for example, said,

> Sunday we played bridge and then went to a coffee shop and had dinner. They're friends, but they're not like the old associates that I had years ago. Now they have their families grown up. Now they have their problems. When my little baby died, I had a friend out and she just jumped right in and did so many things for me. "I'll never forget you for this," I told her and she said, "Oh, what are friends for." That sort of attitude. . . . But of all the friends I have now, I don't know of one . . .

Another spoke of her friend of 50 years: "We can trust each other, and that's something. You don't find many people you can trust. I have many acquaintances, but I have very few friends." A third woman explained, "When you're younger you have friends, but as you get older they move away or die or something. . . . And then you make new friends. You have to make new friends, but I don't think there is quite the same feeling as you have with old friends." Still another described someone who was a friend, not a mere acquaintance: "I am closer to her than I am to my sister because we were together when we raised our children and through the Depression." One woman, who by chance had met a friend whom she had not seen for many years and talked with her for "a long time," remembered the day with wonder: "I was happy all day!" These women seemed to say that only if relationships established by early adulthood were maintained would friends rather than acquaintances be available in old age.

Reviewing the literature to see whether anyone could corroborate the assertion that after a point in life the quality of newly acquired friends was lacking, I found nothing that shed light on this issue. There is almost no research that grounds friendships in the context of social actors' biographies. The process of friendship through the life course and the quality of friend relationships acquired at different points in time have not been addressed, except by those who suggest that they are important issues.

Research on friendships has been exclusively cross-sectional, although in a few studies age groups have been compared in an attempt to uncover variations in number and functions of friends in different stages of the life cycle (Candy, 1976; C. S. Fischer, 1982; Lowenthal et al., 1975). That individuals' friendships exist through time, often transcending spatial boundaries, is acknowledged (Babchuk and Bates, 1963); but most often research questions have been formulated in such a way that respondents' friendships are required, in Claude S. Fischer's words (1982), to be "active" rather than "latent." Apart from allowing respondents initially to identify their friends, no research has focused on the meaning and process of friendships throughout life from the perspective of social actors. Instead, the focus has been on the relationship at one point in time between objective characteristics of friends and respondents such as the number and availability of friends, social integration (Rosow, 1967), morale (Arling, 1976), and mental health (Lowenthal and Haven, 1968), and on the degree of similarity between respondents and identified friends (Blau, 1961; Laumann, 1966; Lazarsfeld and Merton, 1954; Verbrugge, 1977). The subtlety of distinction between old and more recently acquired friends made by the women cited above is lost in existing research. There is simply none that attempts to discover the place of friendship through the life course.

In order to fill this gap to which the informants had led me, I conceived of a research project that had the broad objective of laying bare the meanings attached to friendships and the process of friendships through the life course. To accomplish this, I chose to conduct with old people "guided conversations" (Lofland, 1971) in which they were asked to relate their biographies using friendships as a constant referent. This method of data collection is similar to the "life history method" (Becker, 1970; Crapanzano, 1977; Langness and Frank, 1981). "Topical oral biographies," however, is a more accurate description of the method employed here because I was not interested in explaining one life or in verifying the information provided. A retrospective study was readily acknowledged to be a substitute for a longitudinal one but at the same time to be "a way to get a relatively cheap, preliminary look at possible relations between earlier and later phenomena" (Hindley, 1979:108). This method of data collection promised to "suggest new variables, new questions, and new processes, using the rich though unsystematic data to provide [what I considered to be] a needed reorientation to the field" (Becker, 1970:425) of research on friendship.

As an introduction to the remainder of the book, this chapter begins with a discussion of previous research on friendship to delineate the unique aspects of this project. Then a description of the data collection process and the informants is provided. The problems with and the promises of retrospective, biographical data in general, and for this particular research project, are then addressed. One of those problems, the peculiar nature of friend relationships, is elaborated next. Last, in order to indicate what is to come, the analytical frameworks used to organize the data are specified.

Research Literature on Friendship

In reviewing the literature on friendship, an inherent obstacle is that there are many different definitions used by researchers who seek to answer varied questions within the disciplines of anthropology, psychology, social psychology, and sociology. Research on friendship covers many aspects of interpersonal relationships. The term "friend" is used casually in everyday conversation to describe a variety of relationships ranging from short-term, superficial ones to long-standing ones to which the persons involved are deeply committed. Consequently, the number of definitions is quite large. Few studies, however, are concerned with the meaning attached to friendship relationships or the process of friendships over time.

Psychological and social psychological studies have been limited almost exclusively to studies of attraction and have addressed questions concerning the characteristics, perceived attributes, and attitudes of persons—primarily college students—who are attracted to one another. Much research has occurred in the laboratory in carefully controlled experiments. However, as Ted Huston and George Levinger (1978:133) point out, "the ongoing relationship defies the manipulation of the traditional experiment."

Out of the laboratory, research has focused on persons living in dormitories, housing projects, neighborhoods, and communities, attempting to delineate the characteristics and accuracy of attributions made to persons in dyadic relationships. Reporting research on relationships among members of two communities, Paul Lazarsfeld and Robert Merton (1954) used the word "homophily" to describe their finding that similarities among persons with regard to age, gender, race, marital status, social class, values, and attitudes are important variables in explaining who is friendly with whom. Focusing on the old, Beth Hess (1972) and Irving Rosow (1967) have shown the importance of. age similarity to persons involved in friendly relations. None of these studies, however, has addressed the meaning assigned to the relationship by the participants, the assumption being that persons who interact regularly are friends.

Much of the sociological literature on friendship builds on the research of Alan Bates and Nicholas Babchuk (1961:182), who define a "close friendship" as a primary relationship that includes spontaneity ("Have you ever done anything with this person on the spur of the moment?") and freedom to make demands ("Have you ever talked to this person about personal difficulties that have made you worry or have been a problem to you?"). Subsequent research has used this definition to address issues relating to the composition of respondents' social networks, which are seen to include kin, close friends, and neighbors (Powers and Bultena, 1976; Shulman, 1975); differences between male and female respondents in different social classes with respect to number of friends and definitions of friend (Booth, 1972); characteristics of persons with cross-gender friends (Booth and Hess, 1974); and the gender of the spouse who most influences the choice of friends for a couple (Babchuk and Bates, 1963). In more recent research, Graham Allan (1979) has provided evidence that this definition of "close friendship" is specific to members of the middle class.

An implicit assumption in this research has been that friends will be available for spontaneous activities and demands. In their research Nicholas Babchuk and Alan Bates (1963) expressed surprise that many respondents numbered among their close friends persons with whom they had little contact because of geographical separation. Studies that focus only on current relationships, however, cannot easily include geographically distant friends, and often they are eliminated initially by the types of questions asked or later in the analysis of data.

Another line of questioning that has been followed in research is related to the functions of friendship. Marjorie Lowenthal and her colleagues delineate six specific dimensions that apply to descriptions of friends, including similarity, reciprocity, compatibility, structural dimensions, role model, and a general category of "other." Similarity was the dimension of friendship expressed most often, and there were almost no differences among the responses of the four age groups included in the research, suggesting that the "functions of real friendships may be established at an early age and maintained throughout life" (Lowenthal et al., 1975:58). Sandra Candy (1976) specifically addressed the functions of friendship for women ranging in age from 20 to 80 by asking each respondent to rate the "importance of ten functions for each of her five closest friends." Factor analysis revealed three independent functions: intimacy-assistance, status, and power, with intimacy-assistance being the most important. There were no age differences. By specifying the number of friends, the possibly erroneous assumption is made that the friends are equally important to the respondent. Both of these studies rely upon the respondent's feelings about current friendships, thereby eliminating those that may have been important to respondents at another time. In addition, the comparison of age groups at one point in time precludes the possibility of understanding the process of friendship as it is affected by individuals' biographies. Longitudinal research on friendships that could take these events into account has not been done.

Thus, in terms of understanding the meaning attached to friendships and the process of friendship through time, there are five major drawbacks in the current literature that the research reported here is intended, at least to some degree, to redress. First, the definition of a friend, the meaning of friendship to individuals, has rarely been the issue addressed. Most researchers have assumed that their own definition of friendship is shared by other members of society, rather than attending to the way respondents defined the term. The variety or ways of being a friend and the meanings attached to the word by various members of society and the same members at different times is largely unexplored.

Second, and related to this problem, the definition and meaning of friendship has been only a secondary issue. Most researchers who have investigated friendships have done so as a stepping stone to an issue that was the major focus of the research—for example, the relation between having a confidant and morale (Lowenthal and Haven, 1968); the composition of social support networks (Arling, 1976; Booth, 1972); power differences between husbands and wives (Babchuk and Bates, 1963); the effects on friendship patterns of perceiving attributes as similar (Laumann, 1969); or the effects of marital status on social participation (Blau, 1961).

Third, as Suzanne Kurth (1970:136) points out, most researchers do not distinguish between friendly relations ("an outgrowth of a formal role relationship and a preliminary stage in the development of a friendship") and friendship ("an intimate interpersonal relationship involving each individual as a personal entity"). Research and reviews of the literature on friendship often lump friends, neighbors, acquaintances, and sometimes kin into one category (Arling, 1976; Hess, 1972; Powers and Bultena, 1976; Riley and Foner, 1968; Rosow, 1967). Clearly, these relationships mean very different things to most people, and if the goal of research is to understand the meaning of friendship, keeping these various types of relationships distinct is important.

Fourth, the great bulk of the literature on friendship focuses on the earliest stages of friendship formation—that is, attraction (Altman and Taylor, 1973; Duck, 1973; Huston and Levinger, 1978; Levinger and Raush, 1977). This aspect of interpersonal relationships is the most easily studied because it can be dealt with in the laboratory, but it is probably the least interesting or significant in terms of the sense that persons make of their lives. Many people are attracted to one another when they meet, but a much smaller proportion become friends or, in Lois Verbrugge's words (1977), "mate."

Fifth, a major gap in current knowledge about friendship lies in the lack of information about friendships throughout the life cycle. Most research on friendship focuses on one point in time. An alternative is research that includes more than one age group, but even then, the research is largely abiographical and ahistorical in that it is not put into the context of either persons' lives or the changing society in which they live. Individuals may consider persons whom they have not seen for years to be their "real" friends. Social actors are capable of comparing a past with a current friendship and evaluating the difference. Interpretations of experiences in the past affect current ones. By examining friendships as they exist at only one point in time, the complexity of the process of friendship through time is largely overlooked.

Recent reviews of the literature all point to the need to investigate friendships within the context of persons' lives. Ted Huston and George Levinger (1978:136) state that future research "will need to gather descriptive data concerning the ways in which friendships are formed, maintained, and allowed to fall by the wayside." Norman Shulman (1975:814) notes, "Some speculation about patterns of changes in close relationships through the life cycle has appeared . . . but as Bott has stated, 'no detailed study of this phase change has been published' " (Bott, 1971:299). Matilda Riley and Anne Foner (1968:570) caution, "In the absence of longitudinal studies, there is little indication whether or not changes in friendship follow as the consequence of changes in other roles." They also note that one of the major research questions that needs to be addressed is, "How do friendship patterns of older people compare with those of younger segments of the population? How do they change over the life cycle?" A number of social scientists, then, are in agreement that research on friendship within the broader context of persons' individual biographies is needed. The research reported here is presented as an admittedly small contribution to our knowledge about the place of friendships within people's lives.

Research Design and Informants

Providing the foundation of this book are the transcripts of tape-recorded, guided conversations collected from 63 informants, each of whom related his or her biography to an interviewer using friendships as the thread. As is customary in qualitative research, the informants were treated as experts, representatives of their culture. The decision to collect biographical overviews from many people rather than detailed life histories from a few was deemed a better strategy for research designed to identify issues within a virtually uncharted area. Focusing on one life, or only on a few, makes it difficult to know what is unique to an individual and what may be more generally representative of the culture.

Unlike research enterprises in which careful choice of key informants may be critical (Tremblay, 1957) or in which only a few members of a given society may participate in the "situation" being investigated and thereby qualify as informants (Lofland, 1971), any mentally alert member of American society who met the age criteria (60+) was considered to be an acceptable informant. She or he was "thoroughly enculturated" and "currently involved" (Spradley, 1979), both in her or his own biography and in American society. However, to ensure variation in biography and social location within the society, informants were recruited through a variety of sources.

The names of 16 of the 63 informants were drawn from a list of students in a program for older adults. Almost no one contacted from this list refused to participate. Those who did claimed to be leaving town imminently for vacations. Six were "volunteered" by individuals who knew the author, and the names of an additional 16 were provided by two different agencies. As these informants were asked directly to participate, they are perhaps the least "contaminated," in that they were not self-selected. The remaining informants agreed to participate in the project after hearing about it in a presentation made to groups of older adults, or after reading about it in a flyer distributed in their residences. These individuals are more likely to have had a special interest in the topic, but the variety of explanations they gave for volunteering indicated that there was no single reason. The 63 informants were divided fairly evenly between men and women. They ranged in age from 60 to 80, the median age being 74.

Most of the informants were apprised of the topic in advance so that they could give some thought to it before the interview. The opening question in the interview guide (see Appendix) was, "Looking back over your life and including the present, who are the persons that you consider your friends?" Each was encouraged to begin with childhood friendships and work through to the present, with prompts from the interviewer who asked questions such as, "How old were you?" "Where were you living?" "How did you meet this person?" "Why do you consider this person to be your friend?" "Do you still consider this person to be your friend?" In addition, the interviewers completed a chronology of each person's economic, educational, occupational, geographical mobility, marital, parental, and family history. Interviewers respected informants' presentations. Questions were asked primarily to encourage the informant to continue the narrative or to provide more detail. Some of the interviews lasted only an hour. Others were much longer, but none was longer than four hours. In addition to the author, three graduate students, two of whom were women in their early 20s, interviewed informants. Most of the male informants were interviewed by a man in his late 20s. The interviews were conducted in 1980 and 1981.

The transcripts were analyzed using the method outlined by John Lofland (1971) in his guide to qualitative methods (see also the second edition published with Lyn Lofland, 1984). This method entails immersing oneself in the data to discover what the important themes are, and then sorting them into the categories that emerge. It took some time before the three perspectives that were used to guide analysis and the presentation of the oral biographies became clear enough to provide a framework for the book, not in small part because of the "slippery" nature of the friendship relationship, a theme that is elaborated below.

The old were chosen as informants for this research because they have a unique vantage point from which to tell about friendships. They have literally a lifetime of experience on which to draw, a panorama dotted with relationships that can be dissected, compared, and evaluated. Thus, using the old as informants not only added but maximized the element of time that necessarily is absent in research that focuses only on current relationships and social networks. The fact that friendships have at least a past, sometimes a present, and sometimes a future is lost in research that focuses only on currently "active" relationships. However, it is probably not lost on the old, who, having passed through most stages in their life cycles, are likely to understand the significance of time (Neugarten et al., 1968). Thus, using the old to inform the research was conceived as an attempt to move away from the "snapshots" of individuals' social networks, which are the outcomes of cross-sectional research designs, toward a picture that would capture the process of friendship through the lives of individuals as they move from birth to death—to study friendships within the context of life events.

Evaluating the Data

Although the problems and promises of using retrospective and life-history data have been addressed by others (Becker, 1970; Bertaux, 1981; L. R. Fischer, 1982; Hareven, 1981; Langness and Frank, 1981), they are examined here as they relate to the use of the "topical oral biographies" collected for this project, focusing on (in order) oral, biographical, and topical. The general nature of these retrospective, biographical data, and the significance of their being provided by old informants are addressed, followed by a discussion of the special problems associated with the nature of the research topic.

THE ORAL ASPECT

It is important to keep in mind that the data obtained are oral—that is, they were *spoken* and spoken *to someone.* Unlike written autobiographies in which authors can "objectify" their "subjective" understandings of their lives (Berger and Luckmann, 1967) in several drafts, the words spoken by these informants could not be rescinded. Clarifications could be offered and were encouraged, but no deletion was permitted. The interview situation required putting into words many previously unstated thoughts and feelings. One informant, for example, described some people as "good friends, not close friends." On hearing her usually unstated qualification, she added, "That sounds sort of snobbish." If she had been writing her story, she very likely would have rephrased this after seeing it in print, thereby eliminating the subtler nuances that she apparently made in her mind. Several informants called or wrote to me after the interview to tell me of people whom they had not remembered to include. For example, one informant wrote,

> This evening I found a semantic problem staring at me. Unconsciously I'd hidden a part of myself from you. A certain aspect of my life was wiped out memory-wise this afternoon, and I was unaware of the omission at the time. Problem: Does the definition of *friendship* include love affairs, or is it limited to nonsexual relationships?[1]

In the letter she identified an additional relationship which had not been included in our "conference," explaining that she was telling me "because I wanted to be honest. Also, I guess, I'd like somebody to know that this little old lady has 'been around.'" Of course, there is no way to know how many others might have thought of friends whom they wished they had included. Had the informants been asked to write their stories, or had there been a second or third interview, the data would have been different—perhaps radically so in some cases.

Furthermore, the informants were not talking to themselves but to interviewers—strangers who wanted to know more about their lives and their friends. Vincent Crapanzano (1977:7) points out that a life history is "the immediate response to a demand posed by the Other and carries within it the immediate expectations of the Other." Gelya Frank (1979:70) makes a similar point, describing the life history as a "collaboration involving the consciousness of the investigator as well as the subject." Theodore Rosengarten (1979:117-118) illustrates these assertions in describing his experience of collecting information in order to write the biography of a living, old man:

> I heard Ned Cobb tell a particular story five or six times to different people. He would vary a mood, add or omit a detail, shift himself from foreground to background to produce the effect he wanted. He had one version for his family, one for his neighbors, one for the traveling salesman, and one for me—and they were all the same story, each told with the personality of the listener in mind.... Yet no version is false, once you know all the versions. Each reveals one of the hats he wore—bystander, soldier, plotter. Each is a step on the way to the next, contained in but not contradicted by his other positions.

The conversations recorded for this project are not nearly as extensive as Rosengarten's. There was only one telling permitted, and that to a stranger whose "personality," at least ideally, served as a looking glass for the self of the informant. It would be a mistake, then, to treat these oral biographies as the only "real" ones that could be told. Therefore, they do not lend themselves well to psychological portraits (Mandelbaum, 1973) or to the more traditional uses to which life histories have been put in sociology (Heyl, 1979; Shaw, 1930).

Granting that the data consist of "stories" that are idiosyncratic to the occasion of the interview does not undermine their utility, however. Part of their value lies in their being oral expositions on the culture of friendship. Using his or her own definitions during the guided conversations in which the label "friend" was applied to many relationships, each informant had to "fine tune" the definition as the interview proceeded, to explain what was meant this time, why this person was or was not a "real" friend, how he or she was different from previously described friends. The interview situation demanded that the informants bring to an objective level their taken-for-granted ideas about friendship, combining personal and cultural reality. In essence, these data—products of conversations between directing, but not demanding, "naive" interviewers, and representatives of the culture explaining their personal experiences of friendship—represent the culture of friendship in American society, at least as it is created and understood by the people who contributed to this project.

THE BIOGRAPHICAL ASPECT

It is widely recognized that personal biographies may not be valid—that they are likely to be distortions of what "really" happened. Anthony Greenwald (1980) argues that "normal" adults have "totalitarian egos" that record personal history in a way "not ordinarily admired by historians." Information gathered by asking individuals to recount past events in their lives, then, is not likely to correspond to "the facts," because a constant filtering process is occurring. The number of years over which the informants were asked to range makes room for many "lapses in scholarship." Therefore, the information provided must be recognized as an interpretation of events from the vantage point of self.

Peter Berger (1963:56-57) identifies reliability as another problem when he points out that "as we remember the past, we reconstruct it in accordance with our present ideas of what is important and what is not . . . at least in our consciousness, the past is malleable and flexible. constantly changing as our recollection reinterprets and re-explains what has happened." The problems with which individuals are grappling in the present, then, make past events either relevant or irrelevant and open to new interpretations. For example, until I asked one informant more specifically about college friends, someone who had occupied an important niche in her life was omitted.

> I had one friend who tied in with all my activities from the 1930s until her death in 1970. That was Florence, Florence Ives. I spent vacations with her, including windjammer and any number of things that I wouldn't think of trying now.

Florence was a friend but a friend who had died and therefore was no longer relevant to this person's present or future. In another case an informant described herself as friendless at the time of the interview, and past friends were brought into the interview to illustrate the contrast between her present and past circumstances. As Leopold Rosenmayr (1981:42) cautions, "the mutual or comparable use of biographies must therefore take into consideration the actual situational and structural foundation of the consciousness of those who produce statements about their past life experiences."

Although each informant was dealing with a unique present-life context at the time of the interview, all were approaching the ends of their lives. If Erik Erikson (1959), Robert Butler (1963), and Victor Marshall (1980) are correct in asserting that in old age there is more psychological pressure to assign meaning to the life as a whole than at other points in the life course, biographies told by the old can be expected to be better integrated—more likely to be "legitimated" (Marshall, 1980)—than those told by members of younger age groups. The biographies provided are not simply "the facts" but an interpretation of them from the point of view of old age, a unique stage in the life course.

Information gathered by asking individuals to recount their biographies, to describe and explain events and relationships from the past, can be described best as "projective documents" (Frank, 1980:164), which, according to C. B. Hindley (1979:106), "refer to the individual's view of previous feelings and attitudes, rather than as clearly bearing a direct relation to what they were in the remoter past." Individuals who may have been considered friends at one point in time may be dismissed at a later date as not "real" friends after all, and thereby not find their way into the interview. Both the biographical and friendship data, then, are edited. What are left are the pieces that are deemed important by each informant *in old age*, pieces that have been woven together into a coherent pattern. In analyzing the data, the danger lies in confusing the interpretation of the facts with the facts themselves. More specifically, the propensity of social actors to use the "teleological fallacy"—that end determines process (Bateson, 1979:66)—must be kept in mind in construing informants' explanations for relationships between past and present events.

THE TOPICAL ASPECT

The topic of these biographies also adds to the difficulty of interpreting the data. An important theme of this book is that friends are not "institutionally related" (Suttles, 1970) in the same way that kin and some nonkin are, at least not in American society (see Eisenstadt, 1956; Pitt-Rivers, 1968; Reina, 1959, for examples of institutionalized friendships in other societies). This creates problems for social scientists, as Graham Allan (1979) explains in his treatise on friendship and kinship:

> Finding out who a person's kin are is far easier than finding out who his friends are, for kinship is structured on the basis of acknowledged and

well-known principles while friendship is not. The mental mappings we carry around in our heads do not include friendship networks as they do kinship genealogies [p. 30]. . . .

Factors external to the on-going relationship play no part in its definition. The term "friend" is only applied to people who have a personal relationship that is qualitatively of a particular sort. It is the actual relationship itself that is the most important factor in deciding whether someone can or cannot be labelled a friend. . . . Thus, it is a relational label rather than a categorical one [p. 34].

In the end, then, friends are people about whom each individual has feelings or emotional attachments that only he or she can know.

Two related problems stem from this. First, identifying current friends can be relatively easy, but recalling past friends may be more problematic because it requires "re-feeling" a bond. Stated simply, friends do not become ex-friends in the same way that, for example, spouses do. Therefore, identifying "number of friends" requires much more mental digging on someone's part than identifying "number of spouses." The old adage, "out of sight, out of mind," is more likely to be applicable to friend than marital or other institutionalized relationships. Problems of recall, then, are magnified by the topic of friendship.

The second problem is comparability. Each informant used his or her own definition of friendship, choosing from a lifetime of relationships those individuals whom she or he felt were "qualitatively of a particular sort" (Allan, 1979:34). These definitions vary not only from person to person but through the course of each individual's life as well. Research in which respondents are simply asked to identify their friends and then to answer questions about each one ignores these differences. The diversity of the meanings of friendship through the life course and the variety of meanings represented by the informants can be discovered in qualitative research because the criteria used are revealed in discussions.

There are basic difficulties, then, in recalling and recounting friendships through the life course. At the same time, discussions of friendships reveal personal lives in a way that talk about institutionalized relationships cannot. Oral biographies focusing on the meaning and dynamics of friendships lay bare the "informal" as opposed to the "formal" structuring of individuals' lives and, to a degree, of the society of which they are an integral part.

Friendship as a Social Relationship

As indicated earlier, collecting data on the topic of friendship poses problems of recall and comparability. This theme is developed further in this section because it is this underlying feature of friendship which poses the greatest problem for both research and conceptualization. In everyday language, interpreting the word "friend" is rarely problematic, but for the social scientist doing research on friendships, this is an immediate obstacle. What do individuals mean when they describe someone as a friend? To address this question, the discussion begins by focusing generally on social relationships in order to delineate the unique aspects of the particular social relationship of friendship.

Max Weber (1978) defines a social relationship as "the behavior of a plurality of actors insofar as, in its meaningful content, the action of each takes account of that of the others and is oriented to these terms" (p. 26). He further specifies that the length of time social actors are oriented is not a criterion: "A social relationship can be of a very fleeting character or of varying degrees of permanence" (p. 28). With few exceptions, then, any face-to-face interaction (and some which are not face-to-face) with two (or more) people can be so described.

From the small but influential beginnings with a few primary caretakers, the number of social relationships in which each individual participates expands exponentially, with each person's set of social relationships becoming increasingly differentiated from his or her age peers at the same time that it grows in size as she or he moves through the life course. By the time someone reaches old age in a modern society, the number of people who have qualified as participants with the individual in social relationships is enormous.

Not surprisingly, in all known societies typologies of social relationships have developed so that each need not be treated as unique:

> The reality of everyday life contains typificatory schemes in terms of which others are apprehended and "dealt with" in face-to-face encounters. Thus I apprehend the other as "a man," "a European," "a buyer," "a jovial type," and so on. All these typifications ongoingly affect my interaction with him [Berger and Luckmann, 1967:30-31].

In everyday life, then, most of the myriad of relationships in which social actors participate are categorized, and not by a scheme originated by each individual. Rather, for the most part, the taxonomy predates the individual's arrival and is shared by members of a particular society. Furthermore, some of these typifications are well-defined and institutionalized while others are more open to interpretation.

This is one of the characteristics of relationships in which Georg Simmel (1950) is interested in his discussion of the dyad. According to him, as an ideal type, the dyadic relationship is sociologically "trivial." By this he means that it is characterized by "absence of a super-personal unit" (p. 129). He regards friendship as being very close to the pure form of a dyadic relationship, because it is a "relation entirely based on the individualities of its elements" (p. 138). A marital dyad is much more removed from the ideal "because of its traditional forms, its social rules, its real interests. . . . Marriage contains many super-individual elements that are independent of the specific character of the personalities involved" (p. 138). In contrast, "triviality" characterizes a dyad that is "inseparable from the immediacy of interaction; for neither of its two elements is it the super-individual unit which elsewhere confronts the individual, while at the same time it makes him participate in it" (p. 126). Friendships, then, are trivial because they have a content set by their "two elements." Beth Hess (1972:358) makes a similar point when she writes that one of the reasons that "friendship has often been judged of only minor interest to social scientists" is that it has been seen "as depending more upon idiosyncrasies of personality than upon regularities of culture and social structures."

Triviality of friendship dyads can also be equated with the absence for this relationship of some of the elements of institutionalization. Peter Berger and Thomas Luckmann (1967) identify a compendium of five interdependent criteria—externality, historicity, legitimation, objectivity, and coerciveness—essential for an institution's existence. These can be used to gauge the degree to which a particular pattern of social behavior is institutionalized. Historicity means that the typification "antedates the individual's birth and is not accessible to biological recollection" (p. 60). Externality means that it "exists as a product of human activity" (p. 52). Evidence that both are present in the friend relationship is found, for example, in Robert Selman's (1981) research on children's definitions of friendship, which appear to progress through identifiable stages. The fact that these changes occur can be interpreted to mean that in a particular society, "children develop until they share the same rules for constructing the world as all other adults"

(Kessler and McKenna, 1978:96). Evidence that legitimation or "ways in which [friendship] can be explained and justified" (Berger and Luckmann, 1967:61) is found, for example, in Herbert Gold's (1973:47) article in a popular magazine in which he argues that friendship matters because "we long for company unobliged by blood. . . . We choose to have friends because we must; else we'll have no hearts, we'll not feel alive."

With respect to friendship, however, objectivity and coerciveness are absent, or at least not well developed, in most sectors of modern societies:

> [Objectivity] means that the institutions . . . are experienced as existing over and beyond the individuals who "happen to" embody them at the moment. In other words, the institutions are now experienced as possessing a reality of their own, a reality that confronts the individual as an external and coercive fact [Berger and Luckmann, 1967:58].

As noted earlier, these are precisely the elements that are missing from the friendship dyad (Allan, 1979). Friendships, unlike kin relationships, lack definitive criteria which may be used to determine their existence.

In addition, the content of friendship is set by the two participants; and social pressures to "conform" according to the "rules," or coerciveness, comes only, or at least primarily, from the members of the dyad. Unlike marital dyads, for example, there are no government agencies to enforce a contract signed by the two friends and no grounds for lawsuits for "injured" friends. Social control is "peculiarly up to each member to accomplish. . . . Because there is only one other member, one cannot 'blow the whistle' on another, calling attention of other members to the offender" (McCall, 1970:27).

Conceptualizing friendship as a social institution is deceptive, then, because to do so makes it appear much more concrete than it is in the world of everyday life, a point made well by Graham Allan (1979:37): "In common usage terms like friend (and mate, pal, chum, etc.) are only vague means of analysis; they serve as resources as well as restraints. People use them as labels and devices for conveying meaning in particular situations, not as rigorous and precise analytical tools." This lack of a universal definition poses few problems for social actors who are content to rely on context to supply meaning and rarely question whether their meanings in fact are shared.

Social scientists, however, have attempted to arrive at clear-cut definitions, in essence, to specify "super-individual elements" or to treat friendship as if it were an institution (Babchuk and Bates, 1963; Kurth, 1970; Lowenthal et al., 1975; Reisman, 1979; Suttles, 1970). As an example, B. Bradford Brown (1981:25), in an insightful conceptual piece on age-related dimensions of friendships, stipulates that friendships are "relationships which are voluntary, mutual, flexible and terminable; relationships that emphasize equality and reciprocity, and require from each partner an affective involvement in the total personality of the other." Collectively the informants' ideas of friendship contained these elements, but no one ran through this list of criteria before deciding whether to refer to someone as a friend or whether his or her implicit assumptions about a specific relationship were accurate.

Applying these criteria to a particular relationship may even mean that the person fails to qualify as a friend. For example, one member of a dyad who consciously keeps secrets from the other, according to the above definition would not be making available the "total personality" and, therefore, would not be a friend. An incident of such a "betrayal" is cited by Myron Brenton (1974:125):

> A magazine editor told me how upset he was when his closest friend, a man he had gone to high school with, withheld from him the fact that he had cancer "until he was practically on his deathbed. I tried to respect that; I know he was suffering and had his own reasons for not telling me, but—it sounds terrible, I know—I was hurt . . . like he'd let me down."

Had this incident never arisen, however, the friendship would not have been "tested" nor the man's assumptions about the friendship questioned. Furthermore, given that the incident did arise, is this man now an ex-friend? Several informants had experienced crises in their lives in which friendships had been tested and found wanting. In other cases, however, tested friendships had survived and were described as stronger than the individuals had imagined. In still others, relationships that had not been considered friendships prior to a crisis were redefined as friendship because of others' unexpected responses.

The difficulty of dealing in social science research with the absence of universally accepted criteria is evident in research in which Lillian Rubin (1981), not content with her informants' subjective evaluations, used her own definition of friendship to assess their relationships. Her work is chosen to illustrate this point not because she is the worst offender (she is hardly that!) but because it includes more personal information than is the case in most reports on the topic, in which the process of forming definitions is not included. In one case she concluded that "the words the informant used to speak about his friendships didn't match his inner reality" (p. 107). In the course of a later conversation that was intended to gather the names of friends whom Rubin might interview, she suggested to him one reason he might have felt "kind of low" following the initial interview:

> "Maybe you didn't feel quite comfortable with everything you told me about your friendships. Maybe they're not as solid as you'd like to think." Silence at the other end of the line for what seemed like a long while, then a sigh, "Maybe you're right." In this instance, I interviewed several of the people this man called intimates in order to check out the stories he told. None of them claimed him among their close circle of friends [p. 108].

The implication here is that this man had no "real" friends or at least not nearly as many as he claimed to have. But is Lillian Rubin's "truth" better than her informant's? Lying behind her discounting his feelings about his relationships is the assumption that there is an agreed upon definition of friendship with which to compare relationships in order to determine whether they qualify. This man's friendships did not meet her criteria, but he felt that they met his. Who is right? The informant, or the social scientist who is comparing the informant's answers to her own ideal-typical definition?

Lillian Rubin's interviewing of those identified as friends by an informant brings in another criterion, reciprocity, which is included in most definitions of friendship (see Brown, 1981). In practice, few studies actually test this assumption empirically. However, what is important here is not reciprocity per se but the belief that there is reciprocity, that the other person also regards the informant as a friend. As Max Weber (1978) indicated,

> The subjective meaning need not necessarily be the same for all the parties who are mutually oriented in a given social relationship; there need not in this sense be "reciprocity." "Friendship," . . . on one side, may well be faced with an entirely different attitude on the other. In such cases the parties associate different meanings with their actions, and the social relationship is insofar objectively "asymmetrical" from the points of view of the two parties. It may nevertheless be a case of mutual orientation

insofar as, even though partly or wholly erroneously, one party presumes a particular attitude toward him on the part of the other and orients his action to this expectation [p. 27].

"Reciprocity," like "involvement of the total personality," may be assumed by either member of the friendship dyad until conflicting evidence is perceived. Of course, "objective asymmetry" has "consequences for the course of action and the form of the relationship" (p. 27), just as "objective symmetry" does. For friendship dyads, the possibility of "objective asymmetry" is much greater than for dyadic relationships that are institutionalized. That is, it is much less likely for someone to assume "mistakenly" that an individual is her or his spouse than that an individual is his or her friend. Friendship relationships may continue through many years without the subjective assumption of "objective symmetry" being tested.

Institutionalized criteria to determine the existence of a friendship are not available, at least not in Western societies, so the existence of one depends on the subjective evaluation of a relationship by at least one of its participants. Therefore, the criteria employed vary from one individual to another and are, at least in part, dependent on the dynamic circumstances of an individual's life course and on his or her interpretations of them. To understand friendship within the context of social actors' lives, then, it is important to attend to their definitions of friendship. Because the data under analysis here consist of guided discussions of friendship through time, the complexity of the meaning of friendship is an important theme in the remainder of the book.

Analytical Frameworks

Advice about the analysis of data collected using the life-history method is available, though meager (Langness and Frank, 1981). Anthropologists and sociologists are able to contribute to social science by presenting a particular life history, revealing a culture from the inside; but topical oral biographies cannot be dealt with fruitfully in this way. The life stories must be presented in such a way that the individuality of the informants is left intact at the same time that the more general and shared aspects of their biographies are illuminated. For accomplishing this, three analytical perspectives—cultural, life-course, and social-psychological—were used to analyze the data. Each is described in turn.

CULTURAL PERSPECTIVE

In order to understand and explain a particular life story, David Mandelbaum (1973:180) suggests examining four dimensions, one of which is the cultural: "Cultural factors mold the shape and content of a person's career. . . . The cultural dimension has to do with expectations and known forms shared by the people of a group, with the cognitive and normative thought they have in common." Although he recommends his framework generally to life-history researchers, because his immediate goal is to explain Gandhi's life, the cultural dimension is not considered important in its own right. Rather, it is the background with which to compare the "social dimension," Gandhi's actual behavior or career, in order to determine what is more generally characteristic of his peers and what is specific to Gandhi. Similarly, Glen Elder (1978:23), in an explanation of the life course as a perspective in research, writes of "institutionalized specifications" which "constitute a framework of social rules, standards of evaluation, and expectations that link behavior to rewards and negative sanctions." For friendship, the cultural dimension or the institutionalized specifications remain largely unknown.

On the broadest level, these topical oral biographies can be used to discover the culture of friendship in American society as "embodied" in old members. Peter Berger and Thomas Luckmann (1967:116) write, "Reality is socially defined. But the definitions are always embodied, that is, concrete individuals and groups of individuals serve as definers of reality." As argued previously, the process of these informants' describing and explaining their friendships to someone else, they reveal the taken-for-granted assumptions on the basis of which they organize these relationships in the course of their daily lives. A careful examination of such taken-for-granted assumptions, then, will disclose at least some aspects of the culture of friendship.

LIFE-COURSE PERSPECTIVE

In the last two decades, social scientists and historians have been concerned increasingly with incorporating into their research frameworks the passage of time, particularly with respect to the diachronic relationship between individuals as they age and the changing societies in which they participate (Elder, 1974, 1978; Hareven, 1981; Lowenthal et al., 1975; Myerhoff, 1979; Myerhoff and Simic, 1978; Nydegger, 1981; Riley et al., 1972). Those who adopt a life-course perspective may examine the "career" of an individual, which is "equivalent to an individual's life history" with respect to "role domains"—most commonly those of "marriage, parenthood, consumption, and work life" (Elder, 1978:22-23). Individuals' careers are compared with the statistical norms created both by their own age peers and by older age cohorts who have preceded them in time.

Both Glen Elder (1978) and David Mandelbaum (1973) write of "turnings" or transitions as important snags in the fabric of individuals' lives, making visible the underlying process: "Such a turning is accomplished when the person takes on a new set of roles, enters into fresh relations with a new set of people, and acquires a new self-conception" (Mandelbaum, 1973:181). The stages in the family life cycle (Glick and Parke, 1965) represent turnings in one domain; work history represents those in another. In relating their life stories while identifying friends, the individuals who participated in this research described turnings in a number of "role domains," and it was possible to examine them in relation to those in the friendship role domain. The oral biographies, thus, lend themselves to discovering the effects of turnings in individuals' lives on the acquisition, maintenance, and termination of friendships. Also significant—in that this is a voluntary, dyadic relationship—are turnings in the lives of those identified as friends.

SOCIAL-PSYCHOLOGICAL PERSPECTIVE

A humanist perspective (Berger, 1963) has guided this research from the outset: Individuals are viewed as social actors who shape their own lives rather than as passive reactors to what life brings, or as mere products of their socialization (Breytspraak, 1984). In John Lofland's words (1974:40):

> People devise, gauge, juggle, and *construct* their actions in situations. Human action in situations does not just happen; it is pieced together and built, thought about and tried out, formulated and reformulated. People . . . *work* at acting in the sense that attention is directed to the process

of deciding whether action is needed, what action is needed, how action is to be executed, the execution of action, and the termination of action.

This view of individuals leads to analysis of the biographies with an eye toward discovering how friendships are constructed and what strategies are employed to deal with the problematics of these noninstitutionalized, voluntary relationships. Individuals choose their friends. How do they make the choice—actively or passively? Do they have many friends, few friends, or no friends? Do friendships adapt to changes in the two individuals through time? Are friends committed to one another? Without straying into the realm of psychology, it was possible to examine these data to identify styles that the informants used to deal with the problematic features of friendship relationships from initiation to termination.

Overview of Book

In the following chapters the three perspectives outlined above are woven together. Sometimes one clearly takes precedence, but at others the three are difficult to separate. In Chapter 2, the social-psychological perspective is used to focus on three ideal-typical styles of friendships. However, the significance of these styles to the acquisition, maintenance, and termination of friendships through time makes the life-course perspective important as well. In Chapter 3, the life-course perspective is used more explicitly to examine the maintenance and termination of friendships. In Chapter 4, the cultural and life-course perspectives are used to decipher the rules governing the significance of age and gender to friendships at different stages of the life cycle. Chapter 5 focuses specifically on old age as a stage in the life cycle that presents unique problems for friendships that are mediated by the style of friendship. The final chapter describes the unique contributions that this analysis makes to a clearer understanding both of friendships throughout life and to the value and limitations of each of the three perspectives.

Note

1. Unless otherwise noted, the material cited is from transcripts of the guided conversations with the informants. Some of the information—for example, geographical

location and occupation—was changed to protect anonymity, but substitutions were chosen with care to avoid distortions. In addition, pauses, repeated phrases, and parenthetical discussions are not included, although sentence structure was left intact. This decision to sacrifice conversational realism, hopefully without misconstruing meaning, was made so that the book would be easier to read.

CHAPTER 2

FRIENDSHIP STYLES

While collecting and reviewing the topical oral biographies, it became apparent that the taken-for-granted assumptions that informants held about the importance and meaning of friendships in their lives varied from one person to the next. Statements made about friendship that were "obvious" to some simply could never have been made by others. Given what has been asserted above—that friendship is a noninstitutionalized social relationship—this is to be expected. In this chapter, the different ways in which the informants approached friendships are elaborated.

For each of the individuals who were interviewed, a picture of his or her life course in relation to the acquisition and termination of friendships was constructed. A straight line representing the life span from birth to the age at the time of the interview was marked at the ages at which important turnings had occurred in the person's life—for example, significant events in childhood, deaths of parents, high school and college graduation, each job, each move, changes in marital status, and retirement. Below the straight "life line," lines representing friends were drawn, each one beginning at the age when, according to the informant, the friendship was established and at the age at which it ended, unless it was still ongoing at the time of the interview. If the friend had died this was noted. These "pictures" made it possible to focus on how many friends were claimed, the duration of friendships, and whether acquisition and termination of friendships were related to turnings in various "role domains" (Elder, 1978). From this analysis and from a careful reading of the interviews, three distinct ways of "doing friendship" (Lofland, 1976), or friendship styles, emerged—independent, discerning, and acquisitive. In this chapter each of these is described. Rather than attempt to explain why these informants adopted different styles of friendship, the concern here is with how they differ from one another and how each affected and continued to affect the social relationships and friendships of those who used them.

The Independents

Because of the way they described friendships in their lives, 13 of the informants were classified as "independent." They did not identify any specific individual as a friend as they related their biographies, even when asked repeatedly to do so. Throughout the interview they talked generally about people whom they knew or had known but would not talk about anyone by name, unless it was a person with whom they currently interacted—someone whom they had met, in most cases, relatively recently. Even then, they were often quick to point out that the person was not really a friend. It was clear that most of them were not isolated people, but instead considered themselves to be sufficient unto themselves. To illustrate this style of relating to people with whom they were not in institutionalized role relationships, but with whom they nevertheless had relationships, their descriptions of people they knew are cited.

Referring to his youth, one man said,

> Way back when we were children, going to school, I made a lot of friends with children, girls and boys. And as long as we were together, we enjoyed ourselves. We went to certain little functions that we had and we were always good friends. I wouldn't say there was any special friend. We just enjoyed what we used to do.

Another described his childhood friends in a similar way, referring to them as the "block bunch" and the "routine bunch." After identifying one boy who had died when he was 18 with whom the informant had "bummed around" in high school, he stated that after that he just "hung around" with people:

> I still do. No one in particular. I just have a number of friends, what you might call good friends, but no one that I would consider outstanding. They're just nice people to be with. They're helpful people. I help them, too, along the line, whatever they want, especially the older people. Somehow, they more or less depend on someone that's a little younger. I seldom turn anyone down. I guess it's my nature to be that way.

When asked by the interviewer if there was one friend who stood out about whom they could talk, one woman replied,

> No, I am a very private person. I always lived by the rule "no explain, no complain." When you say too much you are revealing too much about yourself. You should retain a little bit of your privacy and thereby you get pride and you get self-discipline. The very private things you keep to yourself.

Aside from her husband, there was no one whom she identified as being close to her except family members. She knew and admired many people and was not isolated, but there simply was no one whom she considered a close friend in the past or in the present.

Another informant said,

> I would prefer to be absolutely independent. There is a certain dependency involved in friendship relationships that I've noticed among my children, a dependency that I'm not very keen on for myself.

He also considered his spouse to be his best and only friend. One man who lived in a retirement complex replied when asked who his most recently acquired friend was,

> Oh, I consider all of them, most all of them, to be friends. There are some that I wouldn't give you a dime a dozen for them. But still you participate in the stuff that we do here. You have to go along with them, but I wouldn't call them friends.

In telling about his earlier life he expressed the same ambivalence:

> Well, in 1923 I started working at a bakery and that was night work so you don't have many friends then. Well, you do and you don't. The only ones you have are the ones that were at work.

Like the other informants cited above, he allowed the situation to dictate who his associates would be. None was singled out as special and, again, he was careful to point out that he was a person who depended on no one. Another man described his associates in the town where he had lived before moving to his present location:

> We had wonderful times there with people that we've never seen since. There were maybe eight or ten of us that used to go to a place where one of

the men had a cottage, but there wasn't a close relationship as friends. It was more just that passing of time in a social way. . . . But reviewing the situation, I really haven't had very many really close friends.

These informants, apparently beginning in childhood, were content to be with people who happened to be available wherever they were. There was no indication of commitment, and they were likely to identify themselves as loners who did not really need people.

One woman began the interview by making a statement that she had thought about and rehearsed:

Let me preface this by saying that I have been thinking a good deal about this since I knew you were going to talk to me about it. And I said, "Well, just how do you make friends?" It seems to me that one way is the neighborhood in which you live. You get acquainted with people. And some of them become your friends and others are just casual acquaintances. And then there is your school. From the time you are a youngster, you make contacts there. Again, it's selective. You pick out people who appeal to you because you have something in common, besides the fact that you are going to school. And then there is the church, another way in which you make friends, but there again, you are selective. But you form friendships because you are doing things together. And then the other things that occurred to me is the professional connections that you have. And then, of course, that makes me think of friends that I made when I was teaching. And what's become of them? Well, most of them have retired like I have and some of them have moved away. Some of them are gone. And then my last source of new friendships is the people that I have met here [retirement community]. And here, you see, circumstances have brought us together, but I'm still selective. I'm not friends with everybody. But I've made some very good friends with people that I never would have had any contact with if I hadn't been part of this group here.

In relating her biography, she remained true to her initial statement. Throughout her life she had allowed circumstances to provide her with friends, with only one singled out by name, a current one. In response to the query, "Do you have friends that you went to college with?" she replied,

No, not anymore. No, those years are so far behind me. I don't seem to keep close friends. The fact that I only mentioned one person here that I would say is a real friend. But, I'm sort of self-sufficient. I don't seem to need people the way some people do.

About a woman with whom she had lived for over a decade, when they both taught in the same grade school, she said,

> I guess we separated when I went to the other school to teach because I wanted to be within walking distance of the campus and, naturally, she wanted to stay where she was. I think that's what caused us to go our different ways.

And of other friends at the grade school, she said,

> When I left, I had to start all over again to get acquainted with people because I didn't see much of those teachers anymore. Some of the depth of your friendship depends on how much you see people and how you are brought together, whether circumstances bring you together or it's altogether a voluntary thing.

These two schools were within three miles of each other. Characteristic of informants who were classified as independent, friendships for her apparently were much more circumstantial than personal and would fall under the heading of "friendly relations" rather than "friendships" (Kurth, 1970) in the minds of many people, including those classified as discerning and acquisitive who are described below.

The specific associates of the independent informants were affected by the various turnings in their lives. They did not acknowledge ever having had a close friendship, so the commitment necessary to maintain a relationship after a turning was absent. As indicated earlier, they simply established ties with those with whom they were proximate. One man, for example, explained how his marriage had affected his relationships:

> You seem to get away from the people you knew, not entirely, but somewhat, and you make new friends, let's say among the married people, married couples. So, of course, the buddies that you chummed around with, you can't do that all the time. You no longer do that. In a sense you can—you can see them and all that—but you can't go out with them as often as you used to. [Did your wife's death affect your friendships?] Yes, you break away from those married people and you more or less start over, the way you were in your single days. Sure, you see the people and talk to them once in a while, but you don't associate with them like you did. People that were married, you break away from them.

The independent informants, then, allowed circumstances to dictate their associations.

Using the independent style of friendship did not necessarily preclude having known people for a long time. One woman who lived in a retirement community said,

> My best friend here runs the shop, and I support her and her work. Her husband is a lawyer, and they used to be in our church years and years ago, and then they went away. I think she's probably my best friend. I didn't see her until the last few years when he retired and came back to town. And then we renewed our acquaintance. [So you were friends at one time and then. . . .] Oh, closer friends now because of the contact. They're close by. And our interests are very much the same. I have them to dinner over here once a week and she has me for dinner.

About another person she had known many years before, she said,

> Now one that I've revived recently is a girl that I was very friendly with at college. I've looked her up. She wrote to me, so now I write to her a couple of times a year.

Typical of those classified as independent, staying in one place, rather than commitment, meant that it was possible for her to have known associates over many years.

About friendships through the life course, one man explained,

> It seems to me certain times of your life you have an opportunity to come close to somebody, whether it's teenage years or younger or older. And they move away or separation comes between you. I suppose you have to consider that as the normal process of growing up. . . . After we got married I can't think of any particular friends off hand, after I was active in medical circles and so on that I had any real close friends. And I don't think I'm such a hard guy to get along with at that, but that is not . . . [I] just never had the opportunity to develop any close friendships.

However, he had spent his life since leaving medical school in the same community, which others might have seen as ample opportunity to establish friendships. For the most part, then, these independent informants left up to chance those with whom they would associate, and this apparently was a pattern that characterized their childhoods as well.

It is going beyond the limits of the data, of course, to argue that the informants' memories matched what "really" happened. Nevertheless, the conviction with which they spoke is a testimony to their belief that they did.

The interview guide was structured so that each informant was asked to relate his or her biography and talk about friends at the same time. Needless to say, when they did not feel that they had ever had real friends, proceeding with the interview was somewhat problematic. In these cases the format was somewhat different, because informants were put in the position of having to explain as they related their biographies why they were not identifying anyone as a friend. In fact, four of them had prepared statements to read to the interviewer. For example, one began the interview by reading the following statement:

> At 76 years of age I realize that I have not made as many close friends as the majority of people for several reasons, as I will explain in my self-analysis.

The absence of friends to whom to refer in conversation led them to expound their own definitions of friendship more so than those who fell into the other categories. In addition, some felt that their position was an unusual one, although almost no one regretted having used this style, as is evident below.

A number of the independent informants applied such idealistic and rigid criteria to friendships that no one qualified. One man attributed his not having or wanting specific friends to an incident in late adolescence:

> I love friends. I love people. But I've been stung by friends, and I could never place myself in the position where I'd say, "Well, he or she is a *very* good friend of mine." I won't let myself get hurt anymore. [Can you say something about that?] Well, it happened when I met my wife. The boys that I used to go around with—we used to play ball. And then, suddenly, just like I say, when you fall in love, your life changes. So I didn't have as much time to give them as I did to give her. I was the catcher on the team, and one day we were supposed to be playing and she was sick, so I didn't go to the ball game. We lost the game. I got blamed for it because I was doing something else. And I couldn't take that. I couldn't do justice to both of them. So I took what I wanted and that's what I went for. After we got married, we spent 55 years together.

About more recent associates he said,

> I love 'em. I got a lot of friends, too, but I don't say they're friends that I would depend upon. . . . I'm my own man. That's what I want to be. . . . Do I have friends now? I have people that I know.

In this case, the informant's criteria for friendship appeared to include absolute commitment and this precluded friendships once he was committed to his wife. There simply was no room for competing relationships. It is interesting to speculate about how different his discussion of childhood friendships might have been had he been interviewed at the age of 15.

When asked who his best friend was, one man replied,

> I have people that I've known for a period of a great many years, but I think friendship is a fairly rare thing in my life. So it would be hard to pick anyone out that was a real friend in the complete sense of the term.

Again, his criteria were so rigid and idealistic that no one qualified as a friend "in the complete sense of the term." It is instructive to compare these criteria with those for an institutionalized relationship. Spouses, for example, are not called upon to demonstrate that they are in fact spouses "in the complete sense of the term." Instead, agreed upon criteria exist so that the quality of the relationship and whether it in fact exists are separate issues.

Another man used a specific criterion:

> I think there was one fellow who I chummed with quite a bit in high school. But I don't believe he had much influence on my life excepting that we were good companions, as boys will be at that age.

To have qualified as a friend, then, this "fellow" would have had to "influence" his life. Being his own person meant that few people—actually no one he could think of—really had influenced him, and during the interview no one was identified as a friend.

In some cases the informants offered explanations for why they had no friends:

> This is a long way from friendship, but you can see that moving that many times I had to leave friends behind and pick up new ones. And my memory

being what it is, I'd be away from a town, moved to a new one, maybe for a few months; and I wouldn't be able to tell you the names of some of the people that I knew there that I was most friendly with.

Many moves during his adult years, then, "explains" why he had no specific friends to include in the discussion. Extensive family obligations was another reason offered:

I don't have too many. You see, I have a lot of family, a terrific amount of family, and I write a lot of letters to family.

Another offered a similar reason:

But I didn't make very many really good friends there because I always had my older brother, and I think probably he took up the slack a lot of times. If I had been there by myself, it might have been different.

One man referred to his family in a somewhat different way to explain why he had had no friends during the course of his life:

Well, I might give you a little bit of background of my family life, which would set things up. My mother and father were divorced when I was about four, and that has made me probably a little bit more of a loner or an individual than I otherwise might have been. I had very few close friends when I was real young. I'm only trying to dwell on this because, as I interpret the whole thing looking back with an adult approach to it, I can see that it kept me from having a close contact; and since I was an individual who was earning his own way as a kid, I just didn't have the time for close relationships all the way through school. As far as high school relationships were concerned, I had some very good friends there but the relationship ended when we graduated. I never kept any of them afterward. They weren't that kind.

Although the woman who came with a prepared speech—her "self-analysis"—to explain why she had had no friends, did include her family, her explanation was much more wide ranging than that:

Psychiatrists will caution people not to become too attached and dependent on one person for companionship because it is so much more painful to bear the void when that relationship has ceased for one reason or another. I experienced that loss when my sister—two years my junior—

married at 18. Because we had been inseparable, I had not developed more friends in my teenage years. At 18, I began my lifetime work for the electric company, retiring after 43 years of employment. Not being flexible, very dedicated to my job, my days began at 5:30 every morning in order to be able to make the 6:30 bus to avoid ever being late at my desk. With this lifestyle I was confined to dating only on Saturday nights. Curfew Sunday nights was 8:30, which made me very unpopular with friends of the opposite sex. The few friends I had developed during my school years were all married at an early age, while my first marriage did not take place until I was almost 30 years old. This fact caused a drifting apart because of the conflict of interests. My marriage only lasted 2½ years, since I continued to work and had no time to entertain or maintain a home for my husband. [Aside:] See, I can't bring out certain friends that I still see; of course, there's one gal that I went to school with that never married and she and I are on the same level because I had no children, though I've been married twice. [Reading:] My father preceded my mother in death by 20 years, at which time I developed a very close relationship with my mother, taking her with me everywhere on a companionship basis, including my job, my out-of-town business trips. Consequently, when she passed away in October 1965, I felt terribly alone again and married my second husband in 1971. Since I had retired from my job in 1967, I felt a little more relaxed and had a little more time to socialize with other married couples during my second marriage. But this continued only five years as my husband suddenly passed away in 1976, and again I felt alone because of a conflict of interest with my married friends. My lifestyle at present is satisfactory as long as I leave my apartment every day, spending time at the senior center, joining classes and attending lectures. I still cannot say that I have any "bosom friends," since I find entertaining too confining to stay home to do it, and refuse luncheon dates, having skipped lunch for the past 60 years, which is necessary to keep my weight down, so I refuse the luncheon dates. In summarizing, the well-known phrase "in order to make friends, one must first be one" does not always apply because so many of us are only "takers" and not "givers." In my opinion, after close observation, there are at least two sure-fire ways of attracting and retaining friends: First, own an automobile and be fortunate enough to be able to continue driving as you grow older; secondly, be active by accepting responsibility of being a chairperson or hold some office in club groups, etc. Become a leader instead of a follower, which I didn't do. This will attract attention to you as a person much admired and sought after.

A complicated set of circumstances, then, precluded and continued to preclude her having "bosom friends."

In summary, to explain why they had no specific friends, the independent informants in some cases indicated that they used very idealistic criteria in deciding whom to call a friend, so idealistic that no one qualified, and in some cases used biographical explanations such as commitment to or the impediments presented by family. The two explanations were not mutually exclusive. The life-course events that "explained" the absence of friends, however, were not different from those of the informants who were classified as discerning or acquisitive. Life events, then, are not adequate causal explanations. Clearly, the development of these styles is rooted in personality and thus beyond the explanatory power of these data.

Lest the reader come away with the impression that "independent" is equated with "lonely," it is important to point out that most of these informants were not isolated or unhappy. Addressing the issue directly one person said, "I know loads of people here, but I wouldn't say they're close friends. They're acquaintances, and yet I feel very happy." Another informant explained, "We have oodles of acquaintances—not that we're such popular people—but we have many acquaintances, friends, but I couldn't term them as being real deep down friends." The woman cited above included in her prepared statement that her life was satisfactory as long as she could "get out every day."

One reason that most of these independent informants were content with their relationships is that they did not expect them to be intense or intimate, but relatively superficial, especially in comparison with the expectations of those with the discerning style of friendship which are discussed below. One informant explained how to maintain smooth relationships:

It took me years to learn this. If you have an argument with a person, and maybe both are right. Maybe they're both wrong. So all right, you might part. At the moment you're very angry, see. But I think a person should be enough, let's say man enough, to go to the person and say, "If I'm wrong, I'm sorry." That's whether you're right or wrong, the very first thing you know, you're good friends again. That happened a couple of times to me. And now we're good friends. And then you usually wind up discussing the matter in a very friendly manner and then everything's patched up. I think that's the way it should be instead of being apart the rest of your lives.

Another explained,

And I'm accustomed to the idea of a close acquaintance. I mean that I find that a very normal way to be.

A woman whose husband had been her best friend described one area of her life in which she missed him a great deal, revealing at the same time what she expected from relationships with others:

> My husband and I, we both loved and enjoyed dinner dances, parties, and then when we took the cruises we were the last ones to get off the dance floor. We enjoyed the music and it wasn't exhibitionism, but we enjoyed the rhythm and all the old-time songs. My husband played on the banjo and he sang beautifully. So we had a lot of rhythm and a lot of music. And when it happened that I didn't have a partner, I just didn't know what to do. And I couldn't go to any affairs; I mean, I just didn't know what to do. A lot of 50th wedding anniversaries I could not attend. I'd send my regrets, I'd send a gift, but I could not physically attend because of the great emotion. So then, about three years ago, I happened to get the book from the recreation board and it said no partners and line dancing and so on. And I said, well, I need the exercise and I need the music, and so that's where I attempted to go. Now I take the dance exercise class, and that gives me my exercise and feeling of music and I don't need to depend on other people.

She is not attracted to the dancing in order to meet people, possibly to acquire new friends to help ease the burden of her loneliness, but because it is a way to meet other needs.

Other independent informants indicated that they purposefully kept their relationships superficial, either because they did not trust people or because they did not trust themselves. As an illustration of the latter, one informant who felt that her life had been less than successful referred to a period in her life when she had tried to do something about it:

> I remember when I was 27 I went to see a psychiatrist. I knew my world was caving in, and that was when psychiatry was in its infancy. But I couldn't bare my soul to him. I did go; I didn't keep up with it.

Unable to "bare her soul" to anyone, she had been a loner all her life; but, unlike others classified as independent, she indicated that she was troubled by it, seeing in herself a flaw that prevented close ties.

The independent informants did not claim to have any close friends. Some of them could not be persuaded to include even one person. When someone was mentioned it was likely to be a relatively recent acquaintance with whom their relationship was far from intimate. Many of these informants had explanations for why they did not have friends, although not all indicated that they felt that justifications were necessary. Apparently, these informants had always depended on the circumstances in which they found themselves to provide them with friendly relations. One is left with the impression that they are surrounded by a sea of people, none distinguished from the others.

The Discerning

All of the 8 informants classified as discerning identified a small number of people to whom they had felt close, people who were very important to them. One woman began the interview by saying, "My two closest friends died quite a long, long time ago."

> I'd say that I formed a very close friendship in high school within a group of girls. . . . and there was a really close friendship with one of these girls. She died in her forties and so that ended that. And then another friend was a close friend in college and I married her brother, so that friendship was maintained. Really, it became a family relationship then, too. But she also died about ten years ago. After we were married, we went to live in New Hampshire and I didn't form any friendships there. Then we moved to Buffalo and I didn't form any friendships there either. And that was sort of hard, not to have any women to talk to. And then eventually we came back here and then I did form some new, close friendships here with two women particularly. But I would say that would be about it. We have a lot of more casual friends, for instance, that we play bridge with and that sort of thing, but not the type of friends that you are totally unreserved or honest with, that you can let down and say how you really feel about something. I'm pretty on guard most of the time with most people.

During the course of the interview, two other nonrelatives were mentioned as friends. One was a "friend of both my husband and me who was a really good friend whom we thought of as family." The other was a college friend who was jealous of her friendship with the woman who later became her sister-in-law. The informant felt that she was forced by the woman to choose between the two, and that this pressure disqualified her as a "real" friend. Both her husband and one of her daughters were described during the course of the interview as friends, which is in accord with Graham Allan's (1979:41) assertion that when kin are described as friends, it is to emphasize the quality of the particular relationship. For this woman, then, there was no question, no gray areas, about who her friends were. She speaks of her friends the same way one might speak of kin, as if there were institutionalized criteria that could be employed to place individuals in the category. In addition, once she had a friend or two, she saw no reason to look for more. Turnings in her life, then, were much less consequential for friendships than was the case for either the independent or the acquisitive informants.

A male informant identified only two men whom he considered friends, both of whom had had "an impact" on his life. About one he said, "We had a lot of interesting discussions over the years." About the other one—his best friend—he said,

> We had a lot of what we considered very serious discussions, you know, about our lives and the future and what our goals might be and that sort of thing. Then he moved, and I used to go down there during the late '30s to see them and we visited back and forth; they'd come up here. We had a lot of interesting times together, had a lot of fun together. He had a good sense of humor as well as a rather keen mind and we had a very enjoyable time. We were very close and had a lot of discussions regarding our lives and friends and books we had read and things of that nature. Well, this went on until '62 or '63, and then they moved to a different city which isn't too far away, but there again, gradually we've lost touch with one another. I've no idea where they are now. I've lost touch entirely.

In summary, he said,

> Other than those two people—they've had the greatest impact. Oh, there were endless people that we knew as one another, but as far as close association, that sort of thing, or having any real interest in one another or real impact on one another's lives, there wasn't anything that close with one another. There are endless people you met, you went out with, out for dinners and that sort of thing, but not what you'd call a close friend. They're more or less a casual type of thing.

This discerning informant, then, described only two men as friends, both acquired when he was in his 20s, each of whom had had "an impact" on his life. Other relationships he found pleasant but not significant.

Another man who was classified as discerning struggled with defining friendship throughout the interview. He knew many men (and at the time of the interview was close to two women), but only one man qualified as "what I would call a true close friendship":

Now this is a man who is seven years older. My brother and I were seven years apart; my brother was seven years older. And this man, we grew up together, so he's known me ever since I was knee high to a duck and, in fact, he and my brother would have to take care of me. There was just the two of us in the family, so when I was about the age of three or four, why they were saddled with me. And this friendship has maintained itself all through the years and that's quite a few years. Now at least a couple of times a year I go to visit him and his wife and they come by here and visit with me.

He gave as an example of someone whom he did not consider to be a friend a man he had known for a long time and saw regularly at meetings of a group he attended:

There's one couple, one who's somewhat my counterpart in the banking business, he and his wife attend this. Now we've known each other a long time, but I don't consider him a friend. I guess there'd be lots of people you'd put in that category. Yes, you are glad to see each other and they know you, but you wouldn't just on the spur of the moment call them up or they call you; their social life might be in an entirely different arena.

Characteristic of the discerning informants, this man made clear distinctions between friends and friendly relations.

One man opened the interview by saying that he was the wrong person to talk to about friendship:

Because I am very suspicious of people. And I have a reason for it. When I was—as you can hear from my accent I was born on the other side. I was born in Germany. When I started on my doctorate I had a colleague. We studied together for the examinations and we were pretty close. I had no idea that he was a Nazi, an illegal Nazi. When they arrested all the Jews, he came to my house and said to me, "Here. I'm from the Gestapo. I arrest you because you make remarks against Hitler." [And he was a friend?] A close colleague I would call it. And then he arrested me and I was sent to a concentration camp, which is not a nice place to be. So ever since then I am very very suspicious about people. So I'm very distant with people now.

Later in the interview he accounted for his not having more friends:

I don't know how valid my experience is, but my experience is that the born Americans will not consort with foreign borns. They do not accept us. In all the years, it is now 40 years, I lived in the United States, we have not one American acquaintance. All our acquaintances—I don't call them friends, they're all just acquaintances—are German people which we met here that we didn't know over there.

He had two friends in the United States at the time of the interview and specific criteria for those who qualified as friends:

A friend in my opinion is somebody who has similar ideas. For me it means he would have to love classical music. He would have to have an interest in art, not in artists, but like to go to museums. Read good books, love nature, somebody you could have a serious talk [with], not just, "How is your car?" "Is your car [a] good running machine?" "How are the children?" and "How do you cook chicken cacciatore?" A serious conversation. People who have common interests with me. There are very few. [Can you think of any?] Oh, yes, this fellow who introduced me to my wife. He's my wife's cousin. We all lived together in New York. We saw each other two or three times a week. We spent our vacations together, which we still do. We went to Europe together. We went to the West Coast together. Every other year we visit. We were there in July. We take long walks together. I knew him before I knew my wife. I belonged to a group, a social club; we traveled together. He's a friend. I consider him a friend. And then I have a friend in Los Angeles. My wife knew her in Germany. She married an American fellow. They lived in New York, too.

This man, then, was classified as discerning because the only people he considered to be his friends at the time of the interview were two people, one whom he had acquired "on the other side" when he was in his early 20s and the other a woman, also from Germany, whom he had met through his wife. Earlier in his life, he had had more friends from the "social club"—one of his close friends who had lived in London had died during the year preceding the interview—but, at least partly due to his experiencing the Second World War in the way that he did, he was, in his words, "very suspicious of people." In addition, he characterized himself at another point in the interview:

I have the tendency never to ask anybody for a favor. I'd rather go without something than to ask somebody. It's fear, fear of being rejected, you know. I don't want to be rejected so I'd rather not ask.

Another person who was classified as discerning described his first friendship, which was with one of his professors in college:

Now what I call a friendship was when I was a young man, going to college and I met a man who was teaching there. Now that was a friendship that developed between an older man and myself. I did a lot of acting in school and he was head of the dramatic department. But I had read a great deal, practically all of the drama of English literature, Norway, Sweden and German. And so we suddenly became very good friends. . . . It was a friendship that has completely penetrated and also changed most of my life. I formulated a lifestyle and a philosophy from this friendship. It gave me a sense of maturity and a little more character than I would have had if I hadn't had this relationship.

About his other relationships in college, he said,

I only had one college friend. I was a loner. Oh, I had a lot of acquaintances and people that I knew in class, but nobody that was very intimate.

He also described a friendship with a coworker that he had had in his mid-30s shortly before and following his marriage:

He was a young man, a very good-looking fellow. And he had a great sense of humor, and he had a great appreciation for many things that I did. I don't think his interests were mine exactly, although he did have appreciation. Anyway, that relationship became very close because of the fact that he was such a joy to be with. We both sort of were able to find each other so compatible. And being young, we never took anything too seriously. We used to drink together and we used to go out to dinner together. And, yes, it was very close. I will say, however, there was not again the involvement of certain personal relations. I never took my involvement, my personal problems to him. Nor did he to me. And strangely enough, when I go back to this young boy I was going to college with, there again we didn't get into that, but it was a kind of joyous relationship, of friendship.

His friendship with an age peer in college and with his fellow worker five years his junior he regarded as not being of the same high caliber as that with his professor. He talked about only one other man whom he regarded as being as close a friend:

Now that friendship I'd just like to say was another friendship that developed a very, very deep, for me—this was after we were married— because of his tremendous love for music. And we used to sit for hours and hours just listening to classical music. He liked a great deal of twentieth-century music and that built up a very, very important relationship. In fact, in the summertime when we all had our vacations, we would all go to the Cape. But this relationship, it was a good relationship. First of all, he mixed a marvelous martini. And that relationship was built on good drinking and good food and good conversation and a lot of good music. And that was a relationship that was based on an interest. However, he died. He died about seven years ago. When I put on a piece of music I immediately think of him, and when I buy a new record I think, "Good God, I wish he was around to hear this."

Although this informant was involved in many friendly relationships, according to him primarily because his wife was a very sociable person, only these two men were the ones that he considered close friends of his. In explaining the difference in relationships, he cited his experience with actors:

At the theater I made a great many friends because you know actors are bound together because of their insecurity. But remember that those friendships were always short-lived because in the theater people just come in or move out. You're very close to a person perhaps for a season; but the next season everybody's gone. You have a new group coming in. But nothing in a close, personal sense. . . . What I'm trying to say is friendship is not an acquaintance. And I think that you have to very, very definitely separate the two.

He had a great many friendly relationships which he enjoyed and was far from being isolated, even though his two close friends were no longer living; but he was classified as discerning because his ideal of friendship was embodied in two distinctive relationships.

Two men described only friendships in childhood or early adulthood, after which time they appeared to have "put away childish things." For example, one described two close friends, the first from childhood, the second from college:

My earliest friendship was with a boy in our home town. And we became very, very intimate. We were raised like brothers. And we continued our friendship as a matter of fact and we went to college together. And shortly after we got to college, he was taken ill and left. We saw very little of each other after that, although I was best man at his wedding. But there was quite a change in his personality. He became a stuffy, successful lawyer and we drifted apart. We saw very little of each other the last few years. . . .

When we were together on more or less infrequent occasions, I saw that the relationship I had had all those years was dead—he was a different person, a different human being. Now whether it was a result of his success, or certain things which I didn't see as a younger person or his marriage, I don't know. . . . We used to go around like twins. We were inseparable. We did everything together. Everything was always as a team and everyone in town regarded us that way.

In college, he acquired another friend:

And I had a very close friendship with a fellow with the same last name as mine. We were seated alphabetically in class and we became very, very close. And that lasted until a comparatively few years ago. And I never thought of it before. I had these two very, very close relationships. They're the only two in my life that were that close. And this one was almost a repetition of the one I had as a child. And this broke up just a comparatively few years ago.

This friend became a successful lawyer and a Presbyterian:

And I visited him a couple of times down there, and once when I was there he asked us to stay over to go to an Easter ceremony. Well, I didn't mind going, but I didn't like his sense of values. This selling of his birthright for a mess of pottage. I just couldn't take it. And of course his gentile wife, who was also socially ambitious, didn't help any. We haven't seen each other or talked to each other in 20 years.

From the perspective of the life course, it is interesting to note that in this man's mind, 20 years was "a comparatively few years ago." Friendships after these were "not as close, but I think, more mature":

We have some friends here and we have some friends in the town where we used to live who we feel very close to, but I think they are healthier friendships. The others became so ingrown.

As an adult, then, friendships as close as those in childhood and early adulthood were "immature" and, apparently, competitive with his marriage. He credited his wife with making him see the errors in his judgment.

The other man cited three specific individuals whom he considered to be friends; two were friends from adolescence, one from early adulthood. He described with warm feeling one of his adolescent friends: "He and I played together. He was, at that time, my very, very best friend." He had stayed in touch with both of these individuals until his early 40s when both had moved west. Included in the interview somewhat reluctantly was an individual with whom he was still in contact. He and this man had taken classes together in college, but he began to think of him, he supposed, as a friend when they both were colleagues in the early years of their professional careers. Among these three there was a clear ranking, with the "very best friend" from adolescence coming first, the other adolescent friend second, and the colleague a distant third. The first, then, was the standard against which the other two relationships were judged. In describing relationships with others in his life, he explained, "I try to be compassionate. I try to have concern. I try to be just to all the people with whom I am acquainted." With no one else in this man's life had he had a relationship which he would describe as friendship. Even identifying the third person as one may have been an artifact of the interview situation. As with the previous informant, the impression is that when this man reached adulthood he had put away childish things, friendships being one of them. During the course of his life, then, he had moved from the discerning style to the independent style of friendship.

Unlike the independent informants for whom others were an undifferentiated mass, the discerning identified, from this pool of others, only a very few people over the course of their lives whom they considered friends. Although not all of these informants had kept these friendships, those who had, valued them highly. With respect to friendships, these informants were the least affected by the turnings in their lives, although some of them, when they reached adulthood, had "put away childish things" and no longer expected to have close friendships. In adulthood, then, they were likely to resemble the independent or, in one case, the acquisitive. This style is the most difficult to maintain through time. It may well be that if the other informants included in this research had been interviewed much earlier in their lives, more of them would have been classified as discerning.

The Acquisitive

The acquisitive are more difficult to characterize than informants who fell into the other two categories. These were people who moved through their lives collecting a variety of friendships, allowing circumstances to make possible the meeting of likely candidates but, then, committing themselves to the friendships once they were made, at the very least for the period of time during which they and their friends were geographically proximate. Unlike the independents, these informants indicated commitment to specific people with whom circumstances brought them into contact: "I'd say there is a core of half a dozen who are very, very special. Then you could take another group of 30 to 50 that we enjoy and bump into occasionally." Unlike the discerning, they were open to acquiring new friends as they met people with whom they felt some affinity:

> In the past three or four years we've met several couples that we see fairly often. Otherwise you become isolated. And the ones that die and the ones who move out of town, unless you make friends you're isolated. You have to make a conscious effort to make friends.

These informants, then, continued to acquire friends as they moved through their lives.

One informant who illustrates well the acquisitive style had five distinct periods into which she divided her life. The first period that she discussed was childhood. She had many school friends, but especially one girl with whom she had "kept in touch for many, many years, until she married a second time":

> We used to be very, very close friends even after we were both married. But circumstances change things. She's moved out to California and has a great deal of money. Her lifestyle is quite different from mine. I hear about her and she about me, but we're not close anymore. I still love her and have many happy memories of our times together.

After she married, she and her husband, a rising young lawyer 8 years her senior, lived in the city and moved in a circle that included other lawyers and their wives, most older than she. Several women whom she had met during this period of her life she still regarded as friends, or did until they died: "They were our closest friends and right straight through until she died about two years ago."

The third period was marked by her move to the suburbs where she reared her four children. She described one friend: "We share lots of happy memories and confidences. I still talk to her. She calls me or I call her, and she came down to visit me last month." Her husband died just as her youngest child was launched, forcing a transition in her friendships which she spoke of with regret:

> The only thing I thought was kind of too bad when I left there was that I had built up a whole life with everything that you could possibly want. And then after my husband's death, I had to work all day long and I couldn't be chasing back to keep track of my old, original friends. That always pained me, hurt me, but there was nothing for me to do but start fresh. I could see that. They went on. They were busy. They couldn't wait. I couldn't. So we both had to break right off.

Her job, which she was offered by a man with whom she and her husband initially had been friends in the early years of their marriage, brought new friendships, one close one with a fellow employee and another with a nurse:

> When my aunt was living in a hotel, the last three years of her life she was paralyzed and was in bed and needed round-the-clock nursing. And one of her nurses, the three-to-eleven one, was this friend. And I used to come right out from my job to see my aunt and have dinner there. I'd have them bring dinner up on a table and the two of us would have dinner together. And we developed a good friendship. Now that was 1957. That's quite a few years. Nearly twenty-five years. And she has been marvelous to me. I introduced her to my friend from work, and we've had many, many good times together.

The final period of her life was the move to a retirement community:

> When I came I was a different person. I was so full of pep, I could dance all night. And when I came in, I didn't know anybody. Oh, I knew one woman slightly through girl scouts and another woman was an old, old friend, but I just met people all along and I made many friends and had something doing all the time.

With four other women who lived in the retirement community, she started an informal club. By the end of her life, then, she had participated in many of what she considered to be friendships, drawn from five distinct periods in her life. At each transition she acquired new friends, but she did not give up the old ones. Instead, she maintained affectionate ties and reactivated them when circumstances permitted. As she moved through her life, then, the number of people whom she considered to be friends grew, because new ones did not replace but added to old ones.

Other informants had not experienced such distinct transitions, especially in adulthood, but saw their lives as comprising relatively distinct spheres from which friends were drawn. One acquisitive informant, for example, after the interview had proceeded apace, stopped to review what had been said "I think, temporarily, that's it. It's church, clubs, school, retirement community, college, childhood. We've touched on all of these, haven't we?" In a similar vein an informant began with childhood friends whom he had met before he was 5 and then moved through each phase of his life—boarding school, college, military service in World War I, settling into a new community, occupation, military service in World War II, career changes, retirement and after—identifying friends. He had kept almost all of his early friends until they died, adding new ones as he advanced in age. These three informants, then, were typical of the acquisitive, who added friends as they moved through their lives and drew their friends from a variety of role domains.

There were differences, however, with respect to how many friends they felt were enough. Some people believed that an individual could never have too many friends. For example, one informant said, "I've always had a sufficient amount of friends but, still, if you have a thousand, you haven't got one too many." True to her word, in the year and a half since her retirement she had met at a senior center a number of new friends with whom she did things like shopping, baking, and going with them to visit relatives in nursing homes. This informant and those like her accumulated many friends because they kept the old while adding the new.

A somewhat different pattern is illustrated by a man who, when asked how many people from his former place of employment he considered close friends, responded,

> Oh, gosh, sometimes it's hard to draw the line between acquaintances and friends, but there must have been, I'd say, fifty or so of them, anyway, that I considered good friends, played cards with, just a lot of companionship.

Needless to say, being committed over time to this many people is not an easy task, as he explained:

> It's kind of hard to keep track of a lifelong friend, because your environment changes. It seems as soon as you go to work the whole

picture is different. You immediately meet new people. Of course, many of those become friends. But then you change jobs—as I say, my first three jobs all lasted about a year. It wasn't much time to grow good friendships. It wasn't until I got to the place where I stayed for 39 years that I got my roots into the ground.

The intensity of his relationships with friends also is reflected in the size of the group of people he considered friends. About his move to the retirement community in which he was living, he said, "I've never made so many friends so quickly in all my life as I made here." Although similar to the independents in that he relied on the situations he was in to provide him with friends, this man was also unlike them in looking for opportunities to engage in supportive ties with others. This informant replaced friends as the circumstances of his life changed.

The acquisitive informants accumulated enough friends to satisfy their own needs. One, for example, said, "I don't feel that I had many friends, but I didn't feel I had no friends." Another said, "I would say I have three lady friends I associate with." All three had been acquired during the 10 years preceding the interview. About one she said,

> Well, I would consider her my best friend. She lives just right across the boulevard from me. I met her when we were taking driving lessons together, about seven years ago. We had never known each other before but there again she's a very friendly person and when I got to class, we would talk, you know, quite a bit when we would see each other at school. And then later when I passed my test, she was one of the first persons that I called to tell her about it. And I think that since then we started to be friends together. Now we call each other every day.

The other two friends, who are not as close, she does not see as often, although she has known both of them longer. As this informant moved through her life, she had close friends; but when circumstances changed for either one of them, the friendship "faded away" to be replaced by another.

The relationship between the acquisition of friendship and turnings for these informants was clear. With respect to terminations, however, there was a major difference which was evident in the figures constructed to represent each informant's life. For some, new friendships were added to the old ones so that an increasing number of parallel lines were pictured as one moved from left to right, from birth to the time of the interview, with the lines decreasing in number only as friends died. For others, fewer friendships were overlapping. Although quite often they continued to be committed to one or two friendships that were formed relatively early in life, they apparently were not as concerned with maintaining those added over the life course. In both cases, however, it is clear that turnings were important events that set the stage for the acquisition of friends.

As noted in Chapter 1, according to David Mandelbaum (1973:181) turnings occur "when the person takes on a new set of roles, enters into fresh relations with a new set of people, and acquires a new self-conception." Especially for the acquisitive, such turnings—moving to new locations, changes in marital status, and new jobs—were used as benchmarks to describe when friends were acquired. One woman, for example, said,

> I met both of them at parties when I first came to Cleveland in 1928. She is still one of my closest friends.

Another reported,

> I've known her now—this happened after my husband passed away—so I'd say I've known her maybe eight years and we're quite close and I see her maybe once in two weeks or so.

One woman spoke of her arrival in a new community after her marriage:

> Okay, my very first meeting, after he married me and we came over here, I went to a meeting of faculty wives. She was there and she was one of my closest friends. And this has gone on since I met her and we have been friends ever since.

One man explained that he had not had friends in high school, but after that:

> I had friends in college, particularly medical school, very close friends. But probably my closest friend I met in training.

A move to a new community also marked new friends for one woman who said,

> Yes, I did have childhood friends. [Do you still keep up with any of your friends?] I'm trying to think. I guess not, but I have the friends I met here when I first came.

The topical oral biographies of these informants clearly show the relationship between turnings and acquisition of friends.

The acquisitive, then, described very different patterns of friendship throughout their lives from those of either the independents or the discerning. Many maintained long-term friendships while adding to them; others replaced friends with new ones when circumstances changed. Not all of the acquisitive, then, had life-long friends. All were open to making new friends, however, and so continued throughout their lives to acquire friends. Turnings often provided that opportunity.

Three distinct ways of "doing friendship" have been elaborated in this chapter. Informants who were classified as independent, discerning, or acquisitive had different friendship patterns throughout their lives and, as evident in a later chapter, in old age. Their patterns of initiation, maintenance, and termination of friendships throughout life were quite different from one another. All social actors take into account past, present, and future in contemplating actions and in understanding social relationships. A major difference among these three styles is found in which period is emphasized. The independent informants lived almost entirely in the present. They associated with people who happened to be available. They did not expect necessarily that relationships would continue. For the discerning, the past was much more significant. The history of their relationships with a few individuals was very important. Those who had friendships in most cases projected them into the future, but those who had lost friends, saw ahead of them a life in which close friendships would not be a part. For some this was seen as tragic, while others apparently were resigned to it, accepting it as "natural." The acquisitive, in addition to having past and current friends, looked to the future as well. They expected and hoped that the friendships that they had would continue and at the same time were open to adding new ones as circumstances presented likely candidates. In the remainder of the book, these three styles continue to be important as specific aspects of friendship are elaborated.

CHAPTER 3

MAINTENANCE AND TERMINATION
OF FRIENDSHIPS

As noted at the beginning of the book, the impetus for doing this research came from old women who indicated that the friendships they had made earlier in their lives were of a different quality than those acquired late in life. This raised the question of whether people actually maintain friendships with the same people over the course of their lives and, if they do, how they go about it. The research literature indicates that old persons' friends are also likely to be chronologically old, but it leaves unaddressed whether the friendships themselves are also old. These topical oral biographies can shed light on this question.

The future of any social tie is uncertain. For institutionalized relationships, however, there are often formal rules governing the conditions under which they are expected to continue and to end. According to the text of the traditional wedding ceremony, for example, not poverty or sickness but only death is a permissible reason to end a marriage, and the law spells out what is expected of each during the marriage. A friendship, again because it is a noninstitutionalized social relationship, continues only as long as at least one—ideally both—of the members considers it to be one. The conditions under which one may decide that it no longer is a friendship is left unspecified and in many cases may be unspecifiable. The future of any friendship is ambiguous, most obviously when it is new and when turnings occur in either of the members' lives. This chapter, then, examines both if and how informants maintained and terminated particular friendship ties throughout their lives.

Maintaining Friendships

To state the obvious, a prerequisite for having old friendships in old age is that they be maintained from earlier in life. To focus on the maintenance of friendships, then, is to focus on long-term ones. The informants maintained friendships in two ways. Some indicated a high degree of commitment to a particular friendship and acted throughout their lives to ensure its survival. Maintenance was also promoted by a number of favorable social contingencies that made commitment less critical to the survival of a particular tie. These were not mutually exclusive but often reinforced one another. Identifying one as *the* reason that a friendship was maintained would be unfounded.

Informants indicated that they were highly committed to some friendships and in some cases had gone to great lengths to ensure that they continued. One woman, for example, spoke of visiting for the last time a friend with whom she had established a tie in childhood:

> Our friendship lasted all the way through the years until after I had been married. She went off to California—she married out in California. We still maintained a relationship and then she developed cancer. The year that she died, my husband and I made a trip out to California because I knew that would be the last time I would see her.

The informant had helped this friend survive a crisis in her life when they were both in their 20s, and they had continued to be close friends. Comparing them with less important relationships, she described additional friends to whom she was committed:

> The others are more deeply rooted. It's almost like, well in a sense it's almost like a wedded state, because you have intertwined your lives so much that you feel a part of them and they feel a part of you—it is almost like a wedding [marriage].

A man cited earlier said that he had known his best friend since he was "knee high to a duck." At the time of the interview they lived approximately five hours from one another and had rarely lived in the same town in adulthood, but they had made a point of visiting at least three or four times a year. In this case, then, considerable commitment was exhibited apparently by both men to maintain the lifelong friendship. One woman said that she had a school friend from the "early grades": "I think there has never been a year when we haven't been together at least an hour or two during the year. It's a good, deep friendship." She also numbered among her friends two women from college, one of whom was a better friend than the other, and two women whom she had met when she moved to a new town in her mid-20s to begin teaching:

> I have a friend here, a friend I met when I first came here. I've known her for 50 years. This friend is here in the nursing care center. Now I see her almost every day. Take her out, too.

This friend and the other she acquired when she moved to town "were probably the two closest friends that I ever had in my adult life." One man said of his "best friend," acquired in college, who had died shortly before the interview:

> His death has just done a very bad job on my emotions. I feel very bad about it, because that's a real friend to have lasted over those many years, you know.

He had spent time throughout his life with this friend, even though they did not live in the same town, and had helped him make important decisions, for example, whom to choose when he remarried. He had visited with him the previous year in Arizona and was "contemplating the possibility" of moving there. For some informants, then, long-term friends were very important.

In some cases these friendships were maintained not by meeting regularly but through letters and, in more recent years, telephone calls. One informant described friends who lived 3000 miles away and had for many years:

> We haven't seen them, oh golly, we keep in touch, but we haven't seen them for 35 years now. But we still write long letters a couple of times a year. They know about our family. We know about theirs. And it's a good, solid friendship from the beginning, from high school, right on through college and marriage and through the years. It's been a good friendship for all of us.

Similarly, another person reported,

> I had some very good friends in my college fraternity. Those, except for my debating colleagues, were my closest friends. None of them happened to settle in my part of the country and our paths didn't cross very much.

We still exchange Christmas greeting with one of my debating colleagues. There were three of us. The other one has since died, but we used to keep in touch with them pretty regularly. Other than the one surviving member of the debating group, I'm not in touch with any others.

In some cases, then, friendships established early in life were maintained through more or less extensive letter writing. This kept the relationship alive and potentially of significance in the future.

A second way in which friendships were maintained required less commitment. Some of the informants' lives were organized either purposely or propitiously so that maintenance of friendships was promoted and at least some of the onus of responsibility was lifted from the two individuals involved in a relationship. Even for the discerning, for whom commitment to a friendship might be assumed to make circumstances irrelevant, they often were important. Of course, in none of these cases can it be known whether relationships would have continued if circumstances had been less favorable. No causal explanations are offered here. Rather, what is evident in the oral biographies are forces operating in modern societies and strategies used by members that promote the maintenance of these long-term, noninstitutionalized ties.

In some cases informants had "home towns" in which they had lived at least part of their childhoods and in which their parents or siblings continued to reside. Visits "home" meant visits not only with relatives but with friends as well. One woman explained, "In the small town in which I was brought up, there are still people that I consider my friends, and I see them only when I visit the town." She made at least annual visits "home" when her parents were alive. One of her sisters who remained in the town had developed health problems so that her visits to the home town were frequent in the decade preceding the interview and she used this as an opportunity to visit childhood friends. Another informant spoke of a friend from the town in which she had grown up:

We studied Latin together. She always came to our house and we had lunch together. We did our Latin together. She did half and I did half and then we exchanged. I wrote to her for a number of years and when I was in town—I go back sometimes to see people in the neighborhood—I went to see her. And then later she moved away and I lost track of her.

Again, this informant was able with very little effort to maintain the tie. Had her friend stayed in the town, the relationship, in all likelihood, would have continued.

One person who had maintained a close friendship from childhood said,

> My parents continued to live in New York so that my wife and I used to visit them every once in a while. And we would always see him because our friendship was very close, always.

In addition, the choice of a retirement home by one of his children was helpful to the maintenance of this friendship:

> Then my daughter and her husband built a house 15 or 20 years ago in Florida for vacations, and he used to go to Florida so we used to see him down there.

Another informant had a long-standing friend whom she saw when she went to New York City "to see my granddaughter." The "incidental" visits to friends, which were a by-product of visiting kin, were a relatively common occurrence. Another reported that, after his friend moved to Cincinnati:

> We'd be back and forth. He'd be up here. His father passed away in the meantime. His mother was still living—she lived up here—so he used to get back and forth to see her.

Since visiting friends was rarely the primary reason for a visit, once someone no longer had relatives in a "home town" or another place that happened to be near friends, maintenance of an "active" friendship sometimes fell by the wayside.

An additional impetus, and perhaps a more purposive one, to friendship maintenance was changing the voluntary nature of the relationship by formalizing it. In high school, one woman, her sister, and a number of other girls had formed a club:

> You know how girls do. One night we were together and we said, "Let's make a little club." And the club disbanded about five years ago. So it was in existence well over fifty years. We celebrated a fiftieth anniversary. There are only four of us still living, but whenever we're down there, those of us who are still alive get together.

By formalizing the friend relationship into club membership, reliance on individual commitment was muted. Another informant who in his late teens had lived in Europe in the years immediately preceding World War

II had formed "a little club" with age peers, both women and men: "It was more than a club. We spent a lot of time together." Although the members were scattered around the globe by the war, they kept in touch with one another. He considered two of the members to be his closest friends and still wrote to about a dozen people: "We make it our business to write around Christmas time so we report to each other what happened during the year." Some individual members had visited one another in the intervening years. One had come from New Zealand to visit the informant and his sister, who also belonged. In the early 1970s, they had held a reunion in Europe to which many of the members had come. Again, by formalizing what were initially voluntary relationships, the total responsibility for maintaining the ties was lifted from the two individuals. Another man described a club formed in adolescence:

> Several of us were leaders out at scout camp. Then we formed an organization—one of the requirements was you had to be an Eagle Scout and a leader at scout camp, and even though that organization is disbanded, we still maintain our friendships.

Throughout his life he had met often with these men and their families. Furthermore, the club democratized their relationships, protecting the informant from the fact that the other members all were more successful in their careers than he.

Alumni groups are another formal way in which to remove from the individual friends the total burden of maintaining voluntary relationships. One informant had been very active in his college alumni association:

> But the friendships I had at college were very close. I don't mean with everybody, but certain people who I knew very well, and our friendships kept up through the years. Not so much by correspondence, but through reunions. There are a few I still correspond with. Some of them every couple of months. But most of the class is dead.

One woman graduated with eight other people from high school. She had lived with one of the members most of her life, although the two women had belonged to different cliques in high school. Together they kept track of all members of the class: "We graduated nine children, and five of us are still living. Or were last week." Another man reported that his relationship with a college friend continued primarily because of what they read about one another in their fraternity's newsletter:

> Well it still goes on, but mostly through the fraternity. I'll see his name in our newsletter and then he'll see something about me and we'll get in touch at times like that more or less. So it's gone on for 45 to 50 years.

Formal groups established early in life in which the identity of specific individuals is important contribute to the maintenance of long-term ties.

Staying in one place throughout life was another contributing factor. When people move often they are much easier to lose. One woman, for example, had lived in the same house since she was 10 years old and had worked in the same place for most of her life until she retired at age 72. Anyone who wanted to could find her easily, and she claimed to have many life-long friendships.

During the time when the informants reared in Cleveland were growing up, the city comprised a number of ethnic enclaves in which residents were expected to band together. One woman who had maintained relationships with childhood friends explained,

> We all lived in the same neighborhood. That whole neighborhood that we were born in, grew up in. We kept in touch once in a while. You know what I mean. School friends, chums. But we don't socialize is what I should say. But we do keep in touch—different weddings or funerals or picnics.

Although the residents of the neighborhood had dispersed, there were occasions for which the former members of the community were expected to come together. Long-term relationships, then, were made easier because it was difficult for people to lose track of one another because of the "strength of weak ties" (Granovetter, 1973). A number of the informants who had grown up in ethnic neighborhoods attended picnics and other events sponsored by ethnic organizations.

Another source of support for the maintenance of relationships that goes beyond individual commitment is being the "pillar" of something, for example, a church or a community. One woman was the only charter member still attending a church that had been founded half a century ago: "There are friends at church. In fact, most of my friends are at church. And then I write letters, I correspond with folks who have been here [members of the church] and were friends while they were here and have moved away." Again, this informant's life was closely tied to the church, and those who had moved away had no trouble locating her. A similar situation was evident in the case of one informant who, because of his position within the financial world, had been a very visible member of the elite within his community. Even though he had moved away from it for a period of years following his early retirement, when he returned he was well known and fell easily into relationships that evidently were on hold during his absence.

The social organization of modern societies is often assumed to impede the maintenance of long-term friendships. Only friends who are committed highly to one another are expected to be able to overcome the odds against their relationship's enduring. However, an examination of these biographies reveals that there are also forces that promote long-term friendships. People may move, for example, but continue to have roots elsewhere. Such things as high school and college graduation classes, in which individuals have mostly weak ties, may help maintain through the years specific strong ties that may have fallen by the wayside without the added support. Persons view the self and, consequently, their lives as continuous, so perhaps it is not surprising that many would expect and act to ensure that at least some of the friendships supporting that self are also continuous.

Reactivating Friendships

Another way in which these informants could boast of long-term friendships in old age was by having known someone earlier in their lives with whom a dormant relationship was reinstated at a later time. The friendships, then, were not continuously active but were reactivated when circumstances changed. These relationships were resources that, once established, resurfaced at a later point in the person's life. One woman described a friend with whom she had a dormant relationship, recently reactivated:

> Oh, there's another friend I've almost forgotten about. This is a friend I'd made when I was on the staff of the church. The minister brought her to me. She had heard him on the radio and she thought that he was the person that could save her from losing her mind because of her alcoholic husband. He listened to what she had to say and in nothing flat he brought her to me for counseling. It made her furious. She didn't want to talk to this old middle-aged social worker. But we turned out to be friends. And she joined the church. She became active in the women's association, helped to start a prayer group, and was terrific really. And then her husband joined AA and got himself a job, so they had to move and we lost track of each other. I hadn't seen her nor heard from her for 20 years. She

turned up again this winter. I'm going to have to ask her how she found out where I was. She may have asked the church. She called me and came by and took me out to lunch. She helped me buy a new bed. Right now she's laid up because she has a bad foot. She's about 70, not as old as I am, about ten years younger, but the same general age group. And that is the kind of friendship that is hard to account for. And I account for it religiously. I think she was sent to me. Now, if I had said that to anybody fifty years ago I would think I was utterly crazy. It just happens.

This friendship, then, which had faded into the background earlier in the informant's life, reemerged.

One informant described a friend she had made in her early 20s:

Sometimes I stop in New York just to see an old friend of mine who is beginning to go downhill. We used to take summer trips together. And she's going downhill now so I occasionally go to see her. She was my supervisor when I was in social work in New York and we became friends. We used to see her and her husband occasionally. We'd have dinner with them. But he's been dead for quite a few years now and, well, let's see, she asked me about four or five years ago if I'd take a summer trip with her. So we started this. We did it for three years, but this past year she just wasn't up to it.

In this case, after the informant's husband died, her old friend asked her to accompany her on vacations. The friendship, essentially dormant for many years, became important again when circumstances changed. One informant described a boyfriend with whom she had lived in the same ethnic neighborhood as a child. His wife had died "over a year ago" after which time he and the informant had begun going out together. Similarly, another woman responded when asked how long she had known her "man friend," "a long time, but we just picked up the acquaintance about a year and a half ago."

One informant described a complex set of coincidental events that brought her into contact with someone she had known in childhood:

I have a neighbor next door. She lives alone as I do. She's 14 years younger than I, but when she came to that house she was 2 years old and I was 16. And her mother and dad were divorced. And so she went to live with her mother in Michigan and stayed there. I didn't see her. But the dad came, stayed here and remarried. And then this girl married and moved to California. And then her husband died. And her dad got very sick. So she sold her home out there and came here to take care of him. And he died. His second wife was very young and glamorous and had her own business; and she became very ill four years later. But she stayed on. They got along fine. And she [the wife] died. And so she said, "Well, I have no other home to go to. I don't want to go back to California." And she thought she'd stay here. So we have been very good friends. And I see her every day and she watches my house because she doesn't work. And she knows she can just come to the kitchen window and call me and I can open the window and call her. She phones me if she thinks she hasn't seen me around.

In this case, a complex set of circumstances brought together again these two women who had known one another in childhood. That one of these women had remained in the same place clearly made the reactivation possible. Another informant described an old friend:

She is just about ready to retire, and the feeling of knowing each other for so many years, that warm feeling is always present whether we see each other frequently or infrequently. We haven't done anything socially because she's still working. But when we were younger we had a group, a club, we had a sewing group. We also had a mahjong group, so you know that we still feel very close as friends. . . . We used to live on the same street.

When her friend does retire, the two women are likely to have a more "active" friendship.

In other cases informants met friends from childhood after long periods of time. In those cases they were often jubilant in recalling the "homecoming," as was this informant:

I have a very close friend over there. I was back in Yugoslavia in 1977. I met her after 30 years. You see, I'd been here for 25 years already and I hadn't seen her for 5 years before I left Yugoslavia, so it was 30 years since we had seen each other. We had a really nice time. I was invited to an event in my home town. It was raining so hard you'd have thought that somebody was throwing water out from buckets. We had such a good time that we walked in this rain and laughed and laughed. We didn't care about the rain; we were too busy laughing. We had both worked in a factory. We talked a lot about the things we had done and the people we knew from those days. Plus our parents were very good friends. We talked about everything. We had lots to talk about.

In this case poor health and lack of money prevented the informant from returning to her home town again. One man reported moving back at age 45 to the town in which he had spent the first 12 years of his life:

I was brought up here and I made many friends in school while I was here. And these friendships, when I came back, I renewed. These were very old friendships going back to our early teenage years. I bumped into people and was invited to lunch and we renewed old friendships with fellows I used to know. And these are the friendships now that got stronger and stronger even while I was in business, and they have continued since my retirement.

In all likelihood he was aided in re-establishing friendships by an older brother who had returned to the town much sooner than he. Another informant described an old friend with whom he re-established contact when circumstances brought the two men together again:

I was very, very close to him for many, many years, but then I thought he got sort of stuffy about the time he got out of college. I had quite a drinking problem later on, so we drifted way, way apart. But now he's back in town because his sister is in poor health and we're back together better than ever.

He also reported stopping to see another friend while he was on business in the vicinity of the man's home:

At one time, when I was about 22, after we'd been in school together for several years, he turned to me and said, "You know, you're my best friend." I don't remember anyone else saying that to me, so it was interesting that after 45 years we got off on an even warmer basis than it had been before.

Friendships established at one point in life, then, may resurface at a later point. It is not surprising that people once attracted to one another still will find one another attractive when they meet again. Because friendships rarely ended on a bad note—a point elaborated in the following section—but were more likely to fade away, there existed the possibility of reactivating them when circumstances again were favorable.

Terminating Friendships

A question that was included to uncover the process of friendships, from their conception to their demise, was whether informants had had friendships that ended. For many informants it was clear that this was not a question about which they had given much thought. Certainly the people with whom they associated had changed through time, but whether that constituted termination was somewhat puzzling. For example, one informant explained, "Friendships have died. Friends have died, but I don't mean that. I mean that friendships have faded away." One person explained, "It isn't that our friendship was cut off because of any animosity or argument or anything like that. It's just we don't see them." Another said,

> I roomed with a college girl who became a very good friend. We were very good friends for quite a few years. Then you get involved in a different life and friends drop you.

One woman described a friend who had been of great help to her during her unhappy first marriage:

> The only friendship that I could say I had was a lady friend that was kind of in the same circumstances as I was in. We grew up together and were married about the same time and we had our first child about the same time and we were divorced about the same time. So we had all that in common. We would see each other quite often, maybe every day, just about every day. When we had the children, up until the time they were, say, about 5 years old, we would see each other quite often. I must say we had that in common, children of the same age and the same problems, I think. [What happened?] Shortly after I was married the second time, our paths, I don't know, kind of went different ways. And she remarried. She was divorced and she remarried and we saw them some, but really not that much. I really don't remember what happened, but I don't think it was anything that happened. We just kind of separated.

One man, describing his high school friends, said, "I would always drop in on them, pass the time of day when I went home to see my parents once a year. That went on for a few years after I was through school, and then they just kind of faded away."

Friendships made during service in the army, either during World War I or II, were often described in a similar fashion:

> So as far as service friendships, we were friends while we were in. I wrote letters for a couple of years to a couple of guys and then just stopped writing.

> I was in the army for four years and had no trouble as far as making friends. When you live with such a large group, there's always one or two or three whom you become very close to. There's one fella, we were very

close, but then after the war—he lives in Iowa, so that we saw each other only once or twice after that. We exchanged letters and Christmas greetings and things like that, but that ultimately died.

In general discussions of friendship, those made between men in military service often serve as examples of ones that are intense while the men are together but quickly fade once they are civilians again. These informants' experiences were no different.

In most cases the informants made clear that, although a friendship might not be active at the present time, it had not ended on a bad note, so there was a chance for revival:

I can't think of any that have ended. I would say that there are probably some that have petered out—there's a little difference. The relationship would still be a relationship when we see each other, but there isn't a closeness, because obviously there are only seven days in a week and you can't see everybody every day in the week, so that you tend to center your time on the people who are the most important to you.

Another informant described college classmates whom he continued to consider friends:

I made many friends there. With one or two exceptions, that's all faded, too. Once in a while, one of them will pass through town and give me a call. We'll have lunch or I could have them out. But that hasn't happened in the last seven or eight or nine years. These have faded out of the picture as I've gotten older and as I've acquired new friendships in my later life, my business life, mature life, military life, and so on.

"Petered out," "faded away," "died," "just separated," are characteristic of the way friendships which were once significant were described. This is hardly the stuff of which soap operas are made, at least as it is related in retrospect.

In some cases informants provided reasons, most often a change in circumstances, for the "death" of a friendship. In fact, it is not the circumstances alone that account for or cause the "fading away," since others maintained friendships under similar circumstances. However, these changes in circumstances in the informants' minds accounted for the "petering out" of the friendship.

I had a pretty good friend I forgot to mention. When I got out of the army we wanted a house of our own. This friend that I met—we had taken a course together before I went into the service—he had this house. When I got out he said, "Why don't you take the other half of the house I'm living in?" I told him that I didn't have any money for the down payment, so he let me have $200. We lived side by side in that house for five or six years. So, I forgot to mention him. He was a pretty good friend. They got tired of city life and moved down to a farm raising cattle. So I would say he was a close friend. I haven't seen him in years. We've thought about stopping to see him on our way down south sometime. I don't know exactly where he is.

Another informant related a similar experience:

I only had three neighbors there. The houses were that far apart, but all three of the men were friends of mine. Two of the men died. I don't know where their wives are. The other fellow moved into town and bought a hardware store and is still there, I think. I haven't seen him since. He was probably a better friend than the other two although the other two certainly were friends.

A man who eventually came to the United States explained the effects of his emigration on his friendships:

Of course, my relations with all my friends were terminated. I still remember them with great affection. If there would be any contact, if there would be some of them still alive. . . . My friendships were very sincere, close, but terminated in my leaving.

Another informant described the effect of mobility on friendships: "But I've moved around so much. Whenever, in this country and in our type of society, when you leave a place you really pull up your roots with you when you go." The problems presented by geographical mobility also were identified by a man when he explained why he did not know where his high school friend was:

We kept in touch for a while. I'd say for about a year. And then all of a sudden, he didn't write to me anymore and he kept moving around all the time like a gypsy. So I just didn't bother. We couldn't keep in touch with each other.

In these cases geographical mobility and distance between friends were cited as reasons for the fading away of the friendship. It is important to keep in mind that, although this "makes sense" to the informants, geographical distance does not in and of itself spell the termination of relationships.

An additional circumstance that was used to explain the gradual termination of relationships was changes in jobs and retirement. A recent retiree described his interaction with former colleagues:

> We meet—the retirees, we call ourselves—we meet once or twice a year for lunch, those who are still here, those who are still alive. We meet downtown in the private dining room of a restaurant and we have a drink and we blabber all afternoon for an hour or two. I enjoy it. But I can see how distant we're all getting. We're all good friends, but we're getting distant because we're all getting older. Their interests are far removed. We had a common interest—the business—at that time, and common problems. Now this is diminished. We no longer have that common interest. As individuals we like each other and we share each other's pleasures and so on, but it's drifting away and I can feel it. And I think they all can, as a matter of fact.

Leaving school was often cited as a change that "naturally" terminated relationships:

> I don't know how true it is in other cases, but this boarding school had people from all over the country, so that when I graduated there were not many that we kept up with.

In another case someone's no longer working in the same field as the informant, as well as her marriage, were given as reasons for the diminished importance of the friendship:

> After she stopped teaching and had a family and there our paths veered. But whenever we met, the friendship picked up again. And we exchanged cards. She usually sent me, at Christmas time, a holiday greeting card.

One woman explained why a friend with whom she had grown up in an orphanage was no longer a friend:

> She had a very strong attachment to her family, so that fulfilled her and I didn't have it. It made her far more independent. She lived with a married sister and brother-in-law and she had a very good family life, so she really didn't need anybody else.

Changes in geographical proximity, marital status, and occupation are all given as reasons for the termination of friendships. None of these, of course, could be used as reasons for the termination of family membership. Sisters who marry do not cease to be sisters. That these kinds of reasons are seen as legitimate ones points to the fragility of friendships. Because there are no institutional supports to sustain them, changes in circumstances work against their continuation.

In some instances friendships ended in a more active way. For example, persons who once were friends sometimes were viewed as having disqualified themselves by doing something that betrayed the friendship, or changed an informant's evaluation of the person. For example, one man described the end of a childhood friendship:

> One kid who was a good friend of mine in my teens, he became a bum. I'd see him every once in a while. The last time I saw him he borrowed five bucks from me. He was AWOL from the Army. He had turned kind of rotten, but he and I were close for a long time.

Another informant described his high school friend:

> My closest friend turned out to be a gypper. He and I went into cahoots and bought an old Model T Ford and he took off with the son of a bitch and I never did see him, never did get paid back. I gave him $22 and at that time, money was pretty good.

About his two college friends, another man said, "One of my roommates is a lifelong friend. The other one became a crook and I more or less scratched him." The latter disqualified himself, as did this informant's one-time friend to whom he had been very close:

> But when a guy changes his faith, of which he should be proud, really, to something else for the sole purpose of social advancement, I just can't buy it. And my friendship just flew out the window.

One woman recounted a recent experience in which someone's insensitivity disqualified her as a friend: "She's revealed something to me about herself that no way could I even talk to her."

Some of the informants related experiences in which they had found themselves on the other side—that is, had been defined as no longer a friend by someone, for what reasons they could not fathom, although they attempted to make sense of it. One discerning informant, for example, had been dropped by someone whom she had considered a close family friend:

> He was really a good friend, we thought, of the family. He would drop in all the time and he would play golf with my husband, but he seemed to be a friend of the family. And then he was transferred not very far away and for some reason or other he stopped coming and stopped calling and stopped in every way seeing us. No reason that we could figure out. It was very strange. All I can think of. . . . Well, he was a strange man. He was brilliant, but strange. And he always seemed to be putting people to a test. Have you ever met people who do everything to make you dislike them just so they can see that you really, truly do like them? But he was so nice and interesting and we enjoyed his friendship a lot, and at least apparently he enjoyed ours because he was here so often. But he went away and that was it.

Another informant was searching for an explanation for a friend's having dropped him:

> And I had one that you wouldn't believe. We were close friends at college. And I think we'd been out of college about 30 years, and there was this big party in New York celebrating something to do with the college and they had this big dinner. And this fellow with white hair and a great big bushy white moustache was there and he committed the unpardonable sin, "You don't remember me do you?" And I said, "No." And he has never spoken to me or written to me since. And the class secretary—I told him about it—and the class secretary has written him two or three times. When my wife died and I'd had these operations and things, the class secretary wrote to him about some of these troubles and said that he was sure that I'd be glad to have a letter from him. And he never came through at all. Now can you imagine bearing a grudge just because of that? My Lord, I wouldn't expect a person 30 years after we'd been to college to remember who I was. So I would call him one that isn't one of the close friends anymore.

A similar case was described by another person:

> She married kind of late and had had a lot of problems. At a very late date she just decided that I wasn't a true friend to her, but I think she was more disturbed than anything. I don't know where she got that idea. We kind of saw each other from time to time, but there was always something in her imagination that somehow I was against her rather than for her. But I

don't feel that it was a loss because when people get too trying for you, it's better.

One man provided evidence that not everyone views geographical distance as a reason to terminate a relationship. When friends moved out of town, he expected to continue the relationship:

> And then the war came. And of course he went off and she moved back to his parents, I think somewhere in Dayton. And that relationship broke. The only time that we ever corresponded was a long letter at Christmas time and once in a while a phone call. And that relationship, strangely enough, just evaporated. Now she died five or six years ago. She was brought up here and that was the last time we saw him. And we never knew exactly what caused this kind of cooling off of the relationship. I'm sure we hadn't done anything. Or said anything. We were as helpful as we could be to her while he was away at the war.

One woman indicated that she felt that changes in circumstances should not affect friendships, although she could find no other explanation for the "cooling" of a friendship.

> I lost one good friend. And I never have really known—I think she resented the fact that I was promoted. I lived with her for a year when I first came here. And she still would see me and speak to me, but there was no warmth there. And I think it's dreadful when you lose a friend, but I did. And I always have thought that it was due to the fact that I was promoted. And she just thought I wasn't going to be wanting to be with her anymore, that kind of silly thing.

None of these informants thought that changes in circumstances were adequate justifications to terminate friendships.

Except for these last instances of termination, most friendships apparently ended not with a bang but a whimper, and at a time when there was a turning in one of the friend's lives. These were relationships that may have been very important friendships at one point but, with time, faded away and, for most informants, were replaced by others. Regrettably, from the standpoint of this research, these are the ones that are least likely to be remembered when oral biographies are being recounted.

Crises

Contrary to Richard Nixon's assertion that "life for everyone is a series of crises," only a few of the informants had experienced crises in their lives that they considered crossroads. When people did experience crises, however, the assumption of the "objective symmetry" of friendships was tested. In some cases, informants who had not given much thought to friendships were surprised to discover that they had some. For example, one informant who had been transferred to a city to which his wife would not accompany him related this experience:

> When I was working in that city, I knew these same two guys who are back here with me now. I had a bad fall on some ice. I broke my wrist and, of course, I couldn't use this hand. These guys visited me in the hospital, and then, since I couldn't drive, why they picked me up and took me to work every day. This one guy would drive me from work to the doctor for X-rays. Both of them. I'll never forget. These same two fellows moved back here also.

These two men were his closest friends at the time of the interview, and he played golf with them regularly. Another informant who was living in a retirement hotel responded to the question, "Has there ever been a time in your life when you had no friends or friends mattered a great deal?":

> I was quite sick this winter, in February and March. I wanted to die. I prayed, "Dear God, please kill me." They didn't like that. I felt like nobody gave a damn about me. I wanted to die. But I didn't win. I lost that one. And after I went downstairs to eat, I found out I had friends. It was really an experience. It really surprised me. I didn't know I had friends. Even people who didn't know I'd been sick asked, "Have you been away? We've missed you."

In a similar vein, a man recounted calling a colleague late one evening to ask to be put up for the night because the sheriff had just served him with divorce papers and he had to leave his home immediately. Because his friend was willing to put a cot in the living room of his crowded home, the informant felt that his colleague had demonstrated true friendship. In these three cases, individuals who were experiencing crises in their lives for which they needed support found it in hitherto untapped relationships.

Other informants told of long-term friends who came through in crises. For example, one man who had maintained a number of friendships from high school with men who had been somewhat more financially successful than he told of a friend's response to the troubles he and his wife faced when he had had a heart attack in his 40s and lost his job: "After my coronary, after we got down near the bottom, one of my scout buddies came to us and offered us money because he knew our circumstances. But we didn't take it. We got by without it." Another informant told of the support she had received from three long-time friends when her son developed a terminal disease:

> They always called me when he was ill. They never asked me because they knew if I wanted to talk about it, I'd talk. But they never questioned me. Because at the time I wasn't always able to talk about it. And they knew if they asked me at the wrong time, they didn't know what they were going to get back. But they knew enough so if I talked about it, they listened. And they're still my friends today. We still call each other up. Now one I call two or three times a week. She was there with me when he died at the hospital. Talking about friendship, those girls have come through. At any time. In fact, my daughter said to me, "You know, Mom, a little bit I envy you. You still have friends yet. Mine I lose."

Another informant became legally blind in her late 50s and was forced to retire from the teaching profession. She describes her friends as having "stuck with me." Her housemate of 50 years "has seen me through my blindness, which was 26 years." Another friend "has taken me to church ever since I lost my sight. Her I would call a very devoted friend." Becoming legally blind, then, was a watershed year in this informant's life. Her friends were provided with an opportunity to prove their friendship, and this informant had been pleased with the outcome.

Other informants were not so fortunate. One woman, for example, also became blind in her 50s:

> My friends, like I said, were a surprise to me. Really, I didn't expect them to wait on me hand and foot or haul me around. Believe me, I didn't. But I did think they'd at least be concerned enough to call to see how I'm doing. Which they don't.

In this case friends turned out to be considerably less loyal than the informant had expected, and she was in the process of establishing new friendships. Similarly, the woman described above whose son had died had been widowed in middle age when her husband died after a lingering illness. She found the responses of her husband's friends disappointing:

> In fact, I can tell you one friend of his that was his best friend. The minute my husband got cancer he never came. He never once came. He never once came to the house. Never once came to see how he was. See, those are hard things for me to accept.

And she found this response repeated with her son's friends when he became ill.

In this chapter the focus has been on the maintenance and termination of friendships in the informants' lives. Maintaining friendships through time meant that informants had old friendships. In some cases they avowed commitment to specific relationships, while in others circumstances were favorable, so that without as much personal effort the ties could last a lifetime. In still others, long-term friendships were dormant for a period of years and then reactivated at a later point. As people move through their lives, then, they are accumulating relationships—people whom they know—that may become significant at some future point. Only in a few cases did informants remember having ended friendships actively. Most often ties simply faded away when changes occurred in a dyad member's life. Passive endings of friendships were usually accepted as "natural," not the friend's fault, so that if the two met again when circumstances were favorable, there were no hard feelings that had to be confronted and resolved before the bond could be reestablished. Crises, however, forced people to show their "true colors," in some cases challenging but in others confirming the existence of "objective symmetry" in the relationship.

CHAPTER 4

THE SIGNIFICANCE OF AGE AND GENDER TO FRIENDSHIP THROUGH THE LIFE COURSE

Both age and gender are important variables in sociological research because of their significance to the social organization of societies. In the research literature on friendship, both cross-gender and age-discrepant relationships have received attention, although interest in the former has been much greater. Most often explanations have been sought for the differences between men's friendships with other men and women's friendships with other women. The thesis is that because men and women are biologically different, are socialized differently, and/or participate differentially in society, their friendships with respect to such things as self-disclosure and supportiveness are dissimilar. In addition, because a high degree of similarity in status characteristics between members of friendship dyads has been shown through empirical research, relationships in which there is dissimilarity in gender have interested researchers who have tried to account for these atypical bonds. Age similarity has received much more attention than age discrepancy. The principal goal has been to explain why persons of the same age have an affinity for one another.

In this chapter cultural beliefs about the significance of both age and gender to friendships are identified. The focus is on rules as shared meanings: "Specific situations may be analyzed in terms of the rules that participants bring to them" (Lofland and Lofland, 1984:73). The rules that govern the conditions under which men and women may be friends with one another are evident in the informants' descriptions. The contribution of the discussion presented here is not in adding to the well-documented fact that people's friends are likely to be the same gender and age as themselves but in showing how this belief is accomplished in everyday life and through the life course. A discussion of the place of age-discrepant and of cross-gender friendships in various stages of the life cycle is presented. A few of the informants did identify older people with whom they had been friends when they were younger, and many identified current friends who were younger than they. What is evident here, however, is that the rules as shared meaning are not well articulated in the culture, so that previous findings that stress the importance of age similarity to friendships may require modification. The importance of friends being the same gender was well articulated by the informants. Marital status, however, made this rule less clear-cut; therefore, it is addressed in a separate section.

Age-Discrepant Relationships

In the natural scheme of things, those who precede a particular age cohort through time disappear and are replaced by those who follow it through time. When people are young, at least in modernized societies, most people are older than they. As people age, a growing number of those around them are younger, while an increasing number of individuals whom they have known—school teachers, bosses, neighbors from childhood—are dead. The young, then, will have relatively more social relationships—although not necessarily friendships—with persons who are older than they; conversely, the old will have more interaction with persons who are younger than they.

In research focusing on structural explanations for who is friends with whom, similarity in age is uniformly found between members of the dyad. Turning this finding on its head, however, it might be argued that age similarity is thought by many to be a necessary criterion for a relationship to be described as a friendship:

> Ours is a society in which friends are often presumed in advance to be age-peers. As a consequence, close relationships may exist between age dissimilars, but they may not be labeled friendships, either by individuals involved or by the researcher. For instance, a close relationship between a younger and older man may be characterized, not as "he's my friend," but "he's my father figure." [Neugarten and Hagestad, 1976:42]

Individuals, then, may hesitate to describe as friendships close, nonkin relationships characterized by age heterophily.

In the course of discussions of current friendships, as the elderly informants attempted to bring in all relationships that were important to them, younger acquaintances were often included. In some cases these were children who were described as friends to emphasize the quality of relationships. In others, however, nonkin relationships with younger people were mentioned as well. They were generally not the first friendships described but came into the discussions nevertheless. Not as common, but included by some informants, were friendships with adults that they had formed in their adolescent years.

For the young, the other member of an age-discrepant friendship dyad is likely to be older than they, adults who are likely to provide guidance, to be mentors. They may also be thought of as surrogate parents. When people are old, their age-discrepant friendships will probably be with younger others to whom they provide guidance or from whom they receive assistance, depending on their needs. In discussing adolescent relationships, a number of the informants reported having been friends with adults. These were, perhaps, the most difficult friends to recall because they required "re-feeling" a relationship that was both no longer available and experienced a long time ago. The older friend was likely to have been dead for some time, and the admiration felt at one time may no longer have been considered the stuff of friendship once the informant had matured.

All of the informants who reported that in adolescence they had had friendships with adults felt that the friends had influenced their lives and were, therefore, memorable. One man who was cited earlier, for example, described his friendship with one of his college professors, head of the drama department, who had "completely penetrated and also changed most of my life." This older friend was not forgotten easily. Another informant described his relationships with a high school teacher and a school administrator:

> I think my best friend in high school days was probably my debating coach. I happened to be interested in debating when I found I wasn't built for football. And I enjoyed him very much. He was quite an inspiration to me. . . . I used to go home once a year to visit my folks while they were still living, and I would look in on him and also on the superintendent of schools there, whom I admired. In fact, he was the one who gently shoved me aside from a school administrative career. . . . I just admired the way he handled himself and his leadership. I thought he was quite a guy.

These were the only two people with whom he maintained contact after he graduated. In choosing people from this portion of his life to discuss, he indicated that he was not sure whom to include: "There you get into the problem of who's a friend. There are a lot of people you get along with all right, in many different relationships." He pointed out that he had been very active in his high school; but as for close friends, these two men stood out from his age peers, none of whom had gone on to college as he had.

When asked about cross-gender friends, one man recalled an adolescent friendship:

> Years ago I had one woman, older than I. Her parents and my parents were very close friends and she was a musician and so am I, amateur. She became a professional. I used to play for her when she was studying singing. And we became very close friends. But she's really the only woman friend that I think I ever really had. And it was a sort of friendship—her mother and father were so close to us that we used to call them aunt and uncle.

It was atypical among the informants to recall having had adults as friends in adolescence although, if they had been interviewed at that time in their lives, they might very well have included adults. As seen below, many of the informants, now in old age, did include people who were younger than they but struggled with how to label them and usually did not speak of them first. Despite the emphasis on youth subcultures and peer groups, most adolescents live in "social arenas" (Moore, 1978) in which many people are older than they. Thus it would be somewhat unlikely for them not to have older friends. In most cases research designs preclude this possibility.

In the middle years, most people are friends with other adults, and age differences do not appear to be as important. By their late 20s, people reach a point at which they no longer identify with those who are younger than they and begin to use as their reference group those who are older. Differences of even ten years may seem trivial, especially if shared circumstances mitigate against their being intrusive. At the same time, because of the relatively structured progression of stages in the life course and age grading, people who are likely candidates for friendship are most often of roughly similar ages. The age of a friend was rarely included in the discussion spontaneously and, when asked, informants usually indicated that friends were about the same age as they, give or take a few years. It was clear that many had not thought about the actual age of a friend when it was similar to theirs.

In the middle years, acquiring friends who were somewhat older or younger depended on the unique circumstances of individual biographies. Some were with persons considerably older than the informants. For example, one informant who had lost many friends within the year preceding the interview described his first job, which was to become his life's work:

> My situation was that I was the newest, the youngest member of the faculty at the high school where I was teaching, and so I was associated with an older group of people. There weren't any other young teachers that went into the school at the same time I did, so I became acquainted and made social contacts with an older group there than would normally be the case. There weren't many people in my age group on the faculty. I was associated with this older group, and that has continued to be the case. And the younger people that came on, they tended to be with their group and I tended to be with that older group. We all retired just about the same time and now we have a retirement group and we see each other every once in a while. We used to have a sizable group; now I think it's down to about 12 this time. And that's sad, too. There's a sadness about when you get older and you see people dying off. Now we've had five deaths in the group of people who taught with me at the high school in the past six months, and it makes a difference to see all those people.

In his middle years, the difference in age had not seemed important, the consequences only becoming apparent in old age. Another person described a similar set of circumstances:

> The initial people they chose for the staff were all mature, successful, retired businessmen generally. These were all mature people, much older than I. And I was "tail-end Charlie," the youngest by far. I made many friends. They're all dead now. They're all dead. They would be in their 90s now.

One woman did not mention younger friends. All the friends she had acquired were older than she, the same age, or only slightly younger—in part because her husband had been older than she:

> I married a man who was eight years older than I, which made quite a difference in my associations. I went with older couples, older people entirely. He was an attorney and quite well thought of. And I made friends of the wives of his colleagues.

In these cases, then, circumstances brought the informants into daily contact on their jobs or in marriage with persons who were older than they. At the time the friendships were established, age discrepancy probably was noted but viewed as unimportant; but near the end of life, the difference in age had a significant negative effect on the probability of their having long-term friends and associates who were still living and in good health.

In some cases informants had the opportunity to meet and form ties with many people who were younger than they because of their occupations or memberships in organizations. Teachers were the most obvious case in point. One informant spoke warmly of two former students:

> When I went to Toledo recently, I visited a girl that I had in school. I had to teach her English. And I went to visit her just a few weeks ago. And I would say she has been a devoted friend over some 50 years. . . . While I was teaching on the south side of town, I had a boy that had been sent to bad boys' school. They sent him back to me because all the teachers there were old except me. And that kid just loved me and I just loved him. He lived with a grandmother and his parents were divorced and so on. And he wanted me to see his report cards so while I was away for a year he sent his card to me. Well, he finally graduated from high school and became a member of the State Department. And I visited him when we were going around the world. That's my boy John.

The age discrepancy between these two students and the informant was not as great as it would be with future students, but at a much later point in her life she had acquired a younger friend. When she retired in her early 50s because she was legally blind, she called the local high school to ask a teacher to find a student to read to her, "and she recommended Mary," who had been coming once a week ever since. The informant was consulted when Mary considered marrying, and she advised her to go ahead:

> Well, she did and I went to the wedding and now she has five children. And I'm their grandmother. So that's a relationship that's lasted. So she's a devoted friend. Almost like a daughter I would say.

The teacher had also recommended another student to assist the informant, and she had been coming just as long. However, the informant did not consider her to be a friend.

Others who had taught had similar tales:

> You see, I've taught off and on since I was 23, and I've always had good friends among my students. I mean they are friends also. They know my

house. They used to come out to my house in groups. I still keep in touch with some students that I knew in the 1930s. I have met their children and in one case, grandchildren. And we keep in touch that way. Maybe once a year the phone will ring and one of them is in town, and we'll try to make up for the time that we've been apart. Talking over old times, talking over what they've done.

Being in contact with students, then, brings with it the possibility of developing friendships with younger people.

Informants in other lines of work also had formed friendships with younger persons met on the job:

I have another friend. She is a young girl. I met her when we were both working in the cafeteria. She takes me to the doctor and is very nice to me. She gives me a ride whenever I need to go someplace.

This young friend, who is "like a daughter," comes daily to give the informant an insulin shot. In turn, the informant counsels her and gives her refuge from an abusive husband. Another informant explained the effects on his relationships of being between two age groups in the business in which he worked:

In the office most of my friends were the accountants and the outside attorneys that were hired to do the actual prosecution work. The only problem there was that these accountants were older than I, so that by the time I retired, none of them was left. They were all dead. So my friends there were the older people.

At the same time, he developed friendships with those who were younger than he and played baseball and cards with them:

This boy was a draftsman in the engineering department, and I got to know him through playing ball with him, bowling with him. I offered this chap a job as my assistant, and so he came to work for me.

Although this "chap" and his younger colleagues were still living when the informant retired, the company had moved its office to the West Coast, which effectively terminated the informant's relationships with them.

Memberships in age-heterogeneous organizations can also promote friendships that are age-discrepant. One informant was the only living charter member of her church:

Most of my early friends have gone on to heaven. They were older than I. I
made friends with older people a lot of the time, and many of them passed
on to their reward. I guess I have more friends in heaven than I have left on
earth.

However, the congregation also included younger people, one in
particular, by whom she was befriended:

She was a high school girl when I first met her, and my children were
small. We didn't get acquainted right away because I was a married
woman with two children and she was a young teenager. And so that's
how long I've known her. It's a long time. The church was started in 1932
and this is 1980, so you see it's almost 50 years. And I've known her for at
least 45 of those 50 years. We used to go on the street car before they took
it off, and we'd meet at church and she used to tell me, "When I get a job
and buy a car, I'm gonna pick you up and see that you get to church. And
you won't have to take a street car and transfer." So I just thought, oh,
that'll never happen; she'll forget it just like everybody else does. But she
kept that promise so faithfully, what else can I call her but a good friend?
And since then she has married, and she and her husband pick me up
every Sunday morning and for whatever special is going on at church.
And maybe I could call her my best friend because she does that for me
constantly.

Biographical happenstance such as being the youngest or the oldest in a
work setting, belonging to organizations in which there is an age mix,
and occupations or jobs that bring people into daily contact with people
of different ages served as the basis for meeting both younger and older
persons with whom to establish friendships.

Another source of younger friends was age peers who provided access
to younger individuals with whom informants became friends. Again, in
all likelihood this is the case for adolescents as well. This issue, however,
has not been explored because the belief that informs research is that
friends must be age peers. One informant described younger friends
whom she had acquired through a close college friend who was no
longer living:

I knew her sister very well, and I've been friends with her nephew since he
was five years old. He's now 60. He and his wife adopted two children.
This is the first year since 1970 that I haven't gone to visit them. I can't do
it now. They have a boy and a girl. She asked me to be her pen pal and we

are still pen pals. Which means that I was taken on as a substitute aunt. And I was adopted by the two adults, so that's a carried-on-through-the-generations friendship.

She described several other "generations of friendship" and then summarized, "So it keeps on keeping on."

One man described two friendships established with children of friends who were no longer living. In one case an old friend from the country in which he was born had left instructions:

> He kind of left a message for his daughter that she should always treat me as a member of the family, and that's what happened. They are very good friends of mine now. We enjoy each other's company. I have been there every year now since 1969.

In the other case, family friendships continued:

> But when my wife was living, we had quite a number of friends of which there are some remnants left. There was one family with two daughters. The younger of them is still alive but she lives now on the other side of town. While she was living near here, we used to see each other almost regularly, several times a month. Now we talk to each other once in a while, but we don't see each other so often. But that was a very close friendship with the whole family.

He lives with his daughter, which may contribute to the maintenance of this friendship.

One woman relied on a friend's daughter for support. The friend, a former neighbor, had died, but the daughter maintained a relationship with her:

> She's not a young girl, she's 69. She keeps up on account of her mother. She takes me out to the country or comes to visit. She brought me home from the hospital and helped me straighten up. She used to live pretty close but now she has moved. She's ten years younger than me, but she keeps up because of her mother.

By establishing ties with members of subsequent generations, individuals continued to have friends even when the friends who had supplied the initial links were no longer living.

As can be seen from the above descriptions, long-term, age-discrepant friendships are likely to be portrayed in kinship terms. One informant described her friendships with a couple and their children:

> One of my husband's coworkers had a party and we went, and there we met a young couple who are about, I'd say, 19 years younger than I am and we liked each other, husband and wife, both husbands and both wives liked each other immediately. We made a point of seeing each other at different get-togethers. Then when they moved not too far away, we would go over there. They liked to play bridge and we liked to play bridge. We would go over there almost every Friday night to play bridge. At the time that we met them, they had one child a year old. Then gradually they had two more children. We had never had any children and because of the fact that we liked children and they were young and didn't have too much money—not that we had a hell of a lot—and because we had the time whereas they would not have the time, we used to take the kids. Oh, we would take them downtown and to different places that we thought children might enjoy.... Over the years I think the children—although at that time they had grandparents—I think they looked on us more as surrogate grandparents. And there's always been a very very very close relationship between the children, my husband, myself, and this family. At the time that one of the girls married, by that time the grandparents had died, and they asked us to be in the wedding party. The children always felt that they could come to us and discuss any of their problems, which they have done. I still see them almost every Friday night. The married daughter, I ride out to her house and go out with her. One of the daughters is going to be leaving the country and she came one afternoon, well, to coordinate her thinking, to ask how I felt about it, what were the pluses, what were the minuses.

Another informant reported a similar relationship with the daughter of a woman with whom she had been "a good friend at one time." The young woman had gone through a divorce and had remarried. She and her husband had had some financial strains, and the informant did things for them that they were unable to do for themselves, such as eating in relatively expensive restaurants. In explaining why they were "almost like family," she said that "her children call me 'aunt,' " they visited in each other's homes, and the husband did things for her like fixing things around the house.

It is worth noting that the discrepancies in age do not cover the whole spectrum. Almost all the younger friends of these old people were over 30, many well above that age. Links to persons considerably younger were few. As the school teachers and other informants retired, they were likely to lose access to settings in which to acquire younger friends. In addition, extending friendships through age peers to members of third and fourth generations requires too many positive links to succeed in very many cases.

To anticipate the next section, it is also of note that at least some of these age-discrepant friendships were cross-gender ones but were not identified when that topic was discussed in the interview. A woman who claimed not to have had any men friends since her courting days is a case in point. She identified as a friend her former student, "my boy John." This example provides evidence for the assertion made below that cross-gender friendships can be "desexualized" by being considered family-like, something that is relatively easy to do with age-discrepant relationships.

Cross-Gender Friendships

If social actors define only members of their own gender category as appropriate candidates for friendship, half of the population—and for older men a much higher percentage—is ineligible. Despite this clear limitation, almost none of the informants cited as friends persons of the the other gender. A question included in the interview guide was, "Have you ever been friends with someone of the other gender?" Depending on the answer, one of the following questions was also asked: "How is/was this different from being friends with someone of the same gender?" or "Why do you think you have never had a friend who was male/female?" In almost all cases it was necessary to ask these questions directly because very few people mentioned any friends of the other gender without being prompted.

Responses to these questions indicated that cross-gender friendships were considered in most cases to be potentially sexual or courtship relationships and, therefore, essentially different from same-gender relationships in important ways. This means that only during specific periods of the life cycle can cross-gender friends be acquired. Before marriage, when individuals are of an age when courtship is expected, cross-gender friends can be made. When a marriage is terminated because of divorce or widowhood, persons again may be open to cross-gender friendships. Generally, then, the probability of acquiring and—as shown below—having cross-gender friends is higher in late adolescence and early adulthood and, again, in late adulthood and old age. There are circumstances, however, that diminish the sexual overtones to make cross-gender friendships more likely at other stages of the life cycle, and these are identified as well.

In reporting the informants' responses, the actual questions that elicited them are included. The way the question was asked differed, because it was included in the "conversation" between each informant and an interviewer. The reader may judge whether the question itself elicited the interpretation that cross-gender friendships are exclusive. The consistency of the informants' beliefs and experiences indicated to me that it was not the questions per se, but rather the cultural meaning assigned to cross-gender relationships that accounts for the uniformity in their responses.

Asked to focus on friendships with men, one never-married woman talked about the period in her life when she considered courtship to be an issue—apparently the last time in which she had had emotionally close relationships with men:

> [Have you had any men that you considered to be friends?] Well, one fellow from my home town, he and I were friends for an awfully long time, but he was Catholic and I was Protestant. My father wouldn't hear of it. [This was when you were in high school?] Yes, and teaching there, too. He was the one I really was closest to. I probably would have married him if there had not been the religion problem. And interestingly enough, the other boy that I was friends with from first grade up through high school, until we had a row, was Catholic too. Oh, there was another man who came to the house, but I just couldn't see him for dust. He was crazy about me but I wouldn't have had him on a bet.

About her life since that time, she said, "I've never been crazy about men, and they've never been crazy about me."

Other informants indicated that the sexual overtones which presumably are inherent in a cross-gender relationship mitigated against friendships with persons of the other gender:

> [Have you ever had any friends who were men?] No, not too much. Number one, any time anyone wanted to do something for me it was because they wanted some sort of pay, and I never could get into a sexual relationship without love, no way, no how. And I guess this is why I've never had what you call men friends. I've had propositions, but not friends per se.

Another woman interpreted the question in a similar fashion:

> [Have you ever had any men friends?] You mean after I was married or after my husband died? [Either one.] No, I don't think so. I had plenty of male attention, but I don't think I had any that I would trust.

A man who had described his wife as his best friend replied to the question: Have you ever been good friends with a woman other than your wife?

> Well, prior to our marriage, of course, I had girl friends that I might have married but didn't. Since I've been married, I've never had any close friendships with other women.

For him, only one cross-gender friend at any one point in time was considered appropriate, which means that such relationships could occur only serially.

Informants who identified current friends of the other gender in almost all cases were either single or had been widowed at the time the tie was established. The relationships were described as more or less romantic. For example, without being prompted one widow referred to two men friends with whom she had had "dates":

> Then I have friends I go out to dinner with. I've got two boy friends that take me out for dinner. We have a very nice relationship and I enjoy it. The only problem was they both wanted to get married and I told them absolutely not. I said, "My husband put up with me and I put up with him. I don't want to get married. I'm fine the way we are." They're looking to get married, fine. Go ahead. But they like my company because I am a joker.

Until these men find wives, the informant may continue to enjoy their company.

After his wife died, one man reestablished contact after a long hiatus with a woman he had known before he was married:

> And finally I have a friend in Scandinavia who is a retired lecturer from the University. She was, I would almost say, a former sweetheart of mine who is teaching there, and we renewed our acquaintance after more than 40 years.

One woman described how she acquired her "man escort," the widowed husband of an acquaintance. He happened to be in line behind her at the grocery store:

> So, I said, "How is your wife?" because I knew that she had been ill and living in a nursing home. And he said, "Oh, she died about two years ago." And I said, "I am terribly sorry. I didn't know that." And he knew that my husband had died. And he said, "Well, I'll call you"; and I said, "Well, that would be nice. We can go out for a walk or something." So he did and he has been my friend ever since. And I'm not interested in romance. I'm not interested in getting things from him.

She finds this male friend very useful: "At night, of course, we can't go out unless we have a man escort, which is nice I have." Although she is not interested in "romance," her friend functions as a faithful suitor.

A widower identified two women with whom he felt "comfortable." About the first one, the wife of a fraternity brother, he said,

> Then he died and my wife died, and then we began to see each other. I sought it out really more than she did, but over the last ten years, yes, I think she'd say I'm a good friend of hers and she's a good friend of mine.

He went on to describe the second:

> Well, here's another of the opposite sex. We met—and most of these are after my wife died, within the last ten years—and this other one that comes to mind, I see her regularly. We met through a club. It's a good friendship. I would say it's close.

Although he had known one of these women most of his life, he acquired them as friends only after his wife died, when the relationships were not competitive with his marriage. Marriage with either of them had been ruled out ("Those that I want don't want me; and those that do, I don't want"), but he now regards them as people whom he admires and with whom he enjoys spending time. If either were to marry, however, in all likelihood his relationship with her would change.

Friendships with members of the other gender that did not lead to marriage were terminated earlier in life, although in some cases they were put aside and resurrected at a propitious time, as was the case for the informant cited above who reestablished contact after his wife's death with a "former sweetheart." This means that for most people—if the informants are representative—there can be no "active" long-term, cross-gender friendships. For example, one woman said in response to the observation, "One thing that you haven't mentioned is friendships with men,"

> Oh, I always had professional friendships with men. The person I loved the most was Mr. Miller. That was real sad because he was real old and he really wanted me to marry him, but he said he couldn't ask his wife for a divorce because they had been married so long. That was one reason I left that place as quickly as I did.

This relationship did not lead to marriage and, therefore, was terminated. Other informants described similar experiences:

> I worked in New York for a short period of time, but that was only a number of months. I didn't make any outstanding friends there, with the exception of one man, and I wasn't interested in marrying him, so we won't consider him a friend.

Another woman explained,

> I guess we only stayed friends about six months because he had other than friendship in mind. He wanted to get married and I didn't.

And a man explained,

> When I was younger, there were several girls that I went with. We were pretty serious. We were going to get married, as a matter of fact, but it just didn't work out that way. And right now there's one lady—we're not serious, but we're friends.

When marriage is ruled out, cross-gender relationships are terminated, at which point—unlike same-gender ones—they become "ex-friends" or not really friends after all.

One man who married at the age of 35 lamented losing contact with two women friends he had known before his marriage:

> Well, the point is, that always hurt me a great deal because I think it's wrong that we should drop relationships like that. This was an interesting person. This is crazy that you couldn't keep up a friendship with a woman. I know that women can become very jealous. . . . We set up these

relationships and friendships and they're going good, and you break them off instead of terminating them with a little bit of intelligence and smoothing them out and perhaps eventually wanting to go back again and pick them up. Of course, I know that you can't live with a wife and two or three other girl friends, but you know what I mean.

This discerning informant was the only one who questioned the cultural proscription.

Once an informant had described or denied having cross-gender friends, each was asked how friendship with someone of the other gender was different or why they thought that they had not had any. Explanations indicate that most informants felt that there is a basic difference between men and women that precludes friendship. The data cited above illustrate one reason that was used by women informants— that is, that men are not to be trusted because they have ulterior motives. Other reasons were also given, either as a direct response to the question or imbedded in more general discussion.

One woman explained that during the last years of her husband's life, he had been ill but "people liked to talk to him still. So men came to our house a good deal to see him and I left him alone because I felt he saw enough of me and needed men talk." Conversation, then, is different when only men are included. Another woman voiced a similar opinion: "I can talk easy to men because I can talk shop, I can talk politics, I can talk cars." One man used the dissimilarity between his relationships with men and women as an example to demonstrate the difference between friends and acquaintances:

Well, to me friendship immediately suggests warmth. Now I can feel that closeness, warmth, toward these men, particularly ones that belong to the club; but I don't feel that same warmth for most of the women around here. I would consider them acquaintances. They're all nice people. No matter where you go around the building, there's always a cheerful "hello" from everybody, and if they don't see you for a couple of days they remind you you haven't been around. But I don't consider the women to be friends. I don't have that closeness, that feeling of warmth toward them. And it's a matter of companionship; also, I think, understanding. With the men in the club, there aren't any of them that I can't sit down with and talk to, and they'll listen. And there aren't any of them that can't talk to me and I listen, too. So we have an understanding there. I hope Dr. Matthews doesn't object to this, but most women just want you to listen; they don't care if you say anything. I found that out in the course of my work. I had these half dozen secretaries or so in the department, and at times they didn't get along with each other, and they'd come in and cry about it. They wouldn't come in to get an answer to any problem. When they were all through talking, they'd thank me for helping them and I hadn't said a word, just listened to them. That's all they wanted.

In this man's mind, there is a clear difference between the two genders that for him precludes warm relationships with women. Another man of a higher social class, who also was living in a retirement community, expressed himself in a similar vein:

I don't particularly want to ask some of the ladies to have dinner with me. I don't feel like it. I'd rather eat with the men.

True to his word, he had helped to found a men's club that met once a month for the dozen or so men who lived there.

In response to the direct question, informants searched for ways to put into words their feelings about the differences between relationships with members of the different genders. One man, for example, explained it quite pragmatically:

I think with the women it's a little more distant. Because, maybe the women—I don't play golf with the women. I don't bowl with them. I mean, I've been over to their houses and they've been over to our house, too, but I think it's a little more distant than man to man.

According to this man, then, women and men occupy different worlds and have "endogamous" social relationships. Another man, hunting for words to explain how friendships with men are different from those with women, fell back on basic differences that everyone "knows" are there:

I think people are always conscious of the opposite sex. But for ordinary socializing—eating together, going to shows or whatnot together—it's similar. Except, I suspect you talk about different things. That's a kind of hard question to pick out. Certainly there are differences between men and women that must come out in various ways.

One man described a female friend he had had in adolescence:

I think there's a little difference in the sexual relationship. She was attractive, and I think if she'd been really unattractive, I wouldn't have been as close to her. And she had a lot of qualities that I liked. She was vivacious, bright, full of life, and we shared a great deal in common. And she wasn't hard to look at. You don't think of that in terms of your relationship with a man. You may not admit the sexual attraction, but as a normal human being, it's there.

Another informant responded as follows to the question of whether he had had women friends: "Oh, yes, lots of them. They're all beautiful and they're well-educated on top of that." In explaining the difference between friendships with men and women, he said,

Well, you don't treat them the same way, I don't think. You don't hold hands with a male where you would with a girl. This might be old fashioned, but when you walk down the street, the fellow should be on the outside while the girl should be on the inside. I believe in helping a lady get into a car, where I wouldn't help a fellow unless he's crippled. Things like that.

One man suggested that women his own age lacked appeal:

I do have some good friends among women my own age, but I had to work like hell to crank up some sexually magnetic, spirited friends my own age. I succeeded.

This he contrasted to two women 30 years his junior—one a replacement for the loss of the other—with whom his relationships were "spirited" and "enchanting" and required no extra work on his part. This informant also was not enamored with men his own age, but for a different reason—he wished that they were less conservative. Clearly men and women were considered "attractive" for different reasons. Another man felt, at least tentatively, that women were not usually qualified to discuss the issues that were important to him in friendships:

I think you're more inclined with men to discuss things and talk about life or your interests, I think to a greater degree than you would with women. And it depends of course on the women that you know or who you get involved with, but I think, my own feeling is, from my experience at least, that it's a greater feeling, oh, I don't know how to word it. . . . But I think you'd have something of more interest, as far as discussions and topics than you would with a woman. Of course, I'm being old fashioned maybe.

These men, then, considered women to be essentially different from men in ways that disqualified them as candidates for friendship.

After reading these statements, it would be easy to come away with the impression that men and women are not part of one another's worlds, and that would be wrong. Men and women—particularly married men and women, as seen below—did spend a good deal of time with members of the other gender—spouses of friends, couples together, fellow employees—as the following pieces of information make clear:

> I think I've got some good women friends, but they're mostly her friends, too, you know? It's not that I was lily-pure or anything like that, but I went all through that service there and I just didn't touch a woman. I can't think of any other women, any women friends, except just our mutual friends.

> We have friends with people that we both were friends with. I don't think she has a set of friends separate from my friends, and I don't either.

> Some friends from the office—I had a secretary that I contact—and some from work that I have lunch with. They've never been to my home, I don't think. So it would be the office, some from church, the wives of friends.

> But I've had lots and lots of good friends who are women in the education field, lots of them. [Is there a difference between friendships with women and friendships with other men?] Oh, I don't think so. I treat all people the same. I really don't like to be sexist in any respect.

These people, however, were not considered appropriate to bring into the conversation until a question about friends of the other gender was asked directly. They may become important resources, however, when someone is widowed or divorced, as was the case for the woman cited above whose "male escort" was the widower of an acquaintance and for the man cited above who had a close relationship with the widow of a fraternity brother with whom he had established a friendship in college. Another informant married a fellow employee after his first wife had divorced him. When circumstances change, members of the other gender who were not considered friends, but who were still part of informants' social circles, surfaced as potential marriage partners and in some cases became spouses.

There were exceptions to the general rules that because they are courtship-like relationships, only one or at the most two cross-gender friends are permissible at any given point in time. Some people did include specific friends of the opposite gender. This occurred in three general ways. In some cases the person was not considered to be a whole person, was discredited in some way. For example, one informant who was blind said that her most recently acquired friend was a man whom she had met at the local senior center:

And you've got to give him credit, too. He was born with a birth defect. He was in a cast so many days. He is very emaciated-looking. He's got Parkinson's disease. His hand shakes. He comes to that center. He's cheerful. He volunteers. He does anything that he can do. Now, it isn't pity, right? But I'm glad I'm not like him. And he's glad that he's not blind. I mean, we talk that way to each other.

As far as this informant is concerned, this male friend is essentially emasculated and thus in a different category from her two would-be suitors. Another woman described a relationship with a man in a similar way:

I had one male friend with whom I wasn't going out. We simply enjoyed chasing around together. I don't think I could ever have confided in him. Our relationship was probably proximity. There was no romantic interest there.

Persons who are the same age but can be ruled out as potential marriage partners may qualify as likely candidates for friendship.

If there was an age discrepancy in the cross-gender dyad or if for some other reason the relationship could be compared with a familial one, sexual overtones could be eliminated so that a friendship could be established. One woman, for example, considered the physician for whom she had worked to be a friend. Even though both had retired and he had moved away, they talked to one another on the telephone, and she had been invited to attend his granddaughter's confirmation. She explained, "When you work for a doctor it's more of a personal relationship." One man described a long-term relationship that had begun during his college career:

She was a lot older than I and it wasn't more than just a good friendly relationship. And she is, out of all the people I've known, I think that she is probably the one with whom I've had the deepest and best contacts, aside, naturally, from my wife.

His reference to his wife indicates that even for relationships that are easy to see in family terms, the potential threat to a marriage is acknowledged.

A handful of informants, almost all of whom were concerned with the depth of their relationships, included in their pool of friends persons of the other gender. One widow served as a confidant for a number of men who were either married to friends of hers or the husbands in couples that she and her husband knew:

> I knew her long before she married him. Her husband, I think, enjoyed her friendship and my friendship with him as much as he has enjoyed a friendship with anyone else. He is able to confide in me a good deal because he has had some emotional problems as a result of the war. He's a very sensitive person and very frequently he would have horrendous nightmares, and he found it possible to discuss these with me, whereas I think he might have found it difficult with many people. . . . That relationship is over 35 years old.

About the husband of a long-time friend who had died in middle age, she said,

> Her husband seemed to feel, too, that he could discuss with me his fears and his problems, and so forth, mainly by telephone. Once in a while he would come over. Of course my husband was still living then, and he would come over and talk. We would see each other infrequently because, having to run a household, he didn't have too much time. At any rate, two years ago he remarried, and I think with second marriages quite frequently there is an up and down period. I've met his wife. . . . And this is one of the things he sometimes comes over to talk about. Periodically on his way home from work he will stop in here and chat for an hour, have a cup of tea or something and then go on home. She knows that he stops here. This isn't any secret—we're not having an affair of any kind. It's simply a matter of a real friendship in the sense that he is attempting to work out his problems by discussing them with somebody else.

One man described a recently acquired friend, a single woman with whom he and his wife spent a great deal of time when they first retired:

> We hooked up with this gal and we just struck it off, just seemed to be on the same wavelength in most subjects, and we did a lot of socializing together—picnics in the park, concerts, and that sort of thing. So, I would say she was the closest friend we've had, of the female variety. My wife's got a lot of close friends that I find congenial and all, but this one came about in a rather special way and I enjoyed it very much.

One man who counted only two men as friends at the time of the interview, when asked if he also considered their wives to be friends, responded,

Of course. He married a lovely girl. And we became such good friends that I wouldn't know the difference that I knew him before I knew her. She's a divorcee but a lovely, lovely girl. In a word, I don't know that there's any difference. We sit down. She talks to me and we have long conversations. They have a lovely son. As a matter of fact, when their son was born I learned on her son how to change a diaper, how to boil bottles, and how to feed the baby so when our boy was born, I showed my wife how to diaper the baby and boil the bottles. So that's how close a friend I am to her.

Although apparently rare, if these informants are representative of the general population, friendship between a man and a woman is possible when the sexual overtones can somehow be mitigated.

In summary, the characteristics of cross-gender friendships are different from those of same-gender friendships. They are most likely to occur early and late in the life cycle because they are presumed to be more or less sexual and, therefore, exclusive. Long-term, cross-gender friendships are rare; when such relationships do not lead to marriage, they are terminated. Exceptions did occur, however, when the informants could "desexualize" the friendships either by disqualifying the other as a "real" member of the other gender or by seeing the relationship as family-like. In only a very few cases, informants reported having cross-gender friendships that were indistinguishable from same-gender ones.

Friendships between persons of different genders are clearly affected by marital status. Since this type of friendship was viewed by the informants as exclusive—so that at any one time a person may have only one friend of the other gender—whether one is married or single is important. A change in marital status, then, had clear implications for cross-gender friendships, and, as shown in the following section, informants' expectations about how they and their spouses should engage in friendships also affected same-gender friendships.

Friendship and Marriage

Although people rarely identified individuals of a different gender as friends, this did not necessarily mean, for at least some of the married informants, that men did not associate with women, nor women with men. For those who were currently or formerly married, there were three orientations to friendship. Some married informants had friendships that did not include their spouses. Others lived by the dictum that upon marriage the two become one, so the couple had friends in common. A third orientation was to consider the spouse to be the only friend. Each position had implications for the likelihood of socializing with members of the other gender which are elucidated here.

Informants who had separate friends described "my" friends and talked about themselves as distinct from their spouses. They were less likely to spend time in the presence of persons of the other gender. Describing her husband, one informant said,

> My second husband was a person that did not have many friends at all. The only friends he had, that I knew of, were his family and the people he worked with, but he never seemed to want to invite them into the home.

About a friend she had acquired approximately six years before her husband's death, she said,

> My husband wasn't that well and he didn't want to do a lot of things, but he didn't mind if I did. So he didn't mind a friendship with a woman friend where he knew I could enjoy myself. That didn't bother him.

Another informant described a similar arrangement:

> My husband doesn't like to go on trips and he doesn't even go to church with us. He's a homebody, but he's very generous with letting me go and not making any fuss about it.

These two women, then, had friendships in which their husbands were not, and apparently did not expect, to be included. Similarly, a man whose friends were men with whom he played golf explained,

> My wife is younger than I am by 10 or 11 years and her peers are the wives of these other fellas about the same age that she grew up with. She knows all my friends and is friendly with them, but she doesn't see them as frequently as I do. I see them frequently; I see them playing golf—particularly in summer. I see them at lunch once a week, a bunch of them, and so on. This fella who just phoned is not a golfer, but he loves to sit by the swimming pool. And my wife and his wife are quite friendly.

Although this informant and his wife know one another's friends, he regards his friends as his, her friends as hers.

Another informant indicated that she and her husband interacted with other couples but that she had a special friend of her own; in fact, the latter friendship is the one that was not interrupted when her husband died and continued until her friend's death:

> We had married couples as friends. I had one woman friend a little bit on the side, my friend that died recently. I had her that I could go to during the day. We lived in the old ethnic neighborhood. We had a group of friends there and we played cards. The men played and the women played poker all the time. I never did. But I still had my friend, like as my daytime friend, you know, out of context, out of the married picture. I still had her as a friend, and in fact when my youngsters would sleep in the afternoon I could run over to her, since I knew my mother was there, just to get a little bit away from the house.

Although she did share friends with her husband, the more significant relationship was separate and her own. One woman who regarded her friends and her husband's as completely separate said of his friends, usually drinking buddies, whom he brought to their home: "Those were his friends and I didn't consider them my friends." In another case the informant had her own close friends as did her husband, which she felt was appropriate. About her two current close friends she said, "They are my friends"; and when the interviewer asked if her husband also had friends that were only his, she responded,

> Well, he had one dear friend that was his friend and he died. That was a terrible gap in my husband's life, and now he has another friend that he plays golf with, but it's not really a close friendship.

She also regarded her friend from childhood who was no longer living as only her friend: "But that was purely on a personal basis between the two of us because it was not like her and her husband and me and my husband; no, it was not."

In some cases informants explained that they and their spouses essentially led separate lives and as a consequence had separate friends:

> And then I became president of the PTA. And I took a course in public speaking, and then I was president of the League of Women Voters in my community and then of the county. I was very active politically. But my husband objected to—he didn't object, he said, "If you want to do

something like that, that's okay, but it's not for me." Because we didn't get together politically, you see.

When asked if she and her husband shared friends, she replied,

Well, they were not his office people. I will say that. He did not want to tangle his home life with his office. He had an executive position, and he just thought the less I knew about it. . . . He was very busy with his work.

This informant and her husband chose to operate in separate spheres and as a consequence did not share friends. Another informant described a similar arrangement that he and his wife had made:

There are a couple of professional associates here that I've known for a great many years. We go to lunch from time to time. But we keep it that way. We don't relate as couples that much. You see my wife has always worked, and we agreed on one thing long, long ago and this is that whatever my work was, she didn't have to be involved in it. You know, the supportive wife in the corporation. We agreed that that would never occur, didn't need to occur. That has worked out well. Because there's no reason why she should have to enjoy the company of the girls that some of my friends married. I mean, there's no reason for that. And she has her best friends at her clubs, and I have my friends that work with me, people like that.

One informant felt that as a husband he was compelled to socialize with his wife, but not necessarily with enthusiasm: "They are my wife's friends. If she wants to see them, I go along. If they come to our house, I accept them."

Informants who were in marriages in which they and their spouses had separate friends socialized almost exclusively with members of their own gender. Having a friend of the other gender clearly was considered to be inappropriate. As the woman cited above said of her husband, "He didn't mind a friendship with a woman friend." Had she chosen to enjoy herself with a man friend, however, her husband in all likelihood would have objected. For informants using this orientation, then, their claim to have had friends of the other gender only before they were married or when they were widowed or divorced is probably accurate. For informants who were couple-oriented, however, relationships were likely to be with other couples. It is somewhat inconsistent that informants did not consider the opposite-gender member of a couple as a cross-gender friend.

Rather than having separate friends, for some informants an expectation accompanying marriage was that they would have joint friends. Once they had married, their orientation to the world was as a member of a couple rather than as an individual, and this included friendships. One woman, for example, married for the first time in her late 30s, by which time both she and her husband, who was approximately the same age as she, had established friendships:

> My husband enjoyed my friends. I made it a point, of course, to enjoy his friends, too. And we never did have any problems in that respect. We shared friends. Obviously when you marry, each one of you has had friends from before. I imagine because the wife ordinarily makes the social contacts, you must make a special effort to include your husband's friends at the outset; then, gradually, they become your friends, too. And then there's no longer a division between "my" friends and "your" friends. It's at the outset of marriage that this occurs. After marriage, obviously, your friends are common friends.

As was made clear above, this was not "obvious" to everyone. In answering the question of whether she and her husband had separate friends or shared friends, one informant, very much like the previous one, explained,

> Now this man who just died, now he was my friend, but he was my husband's friend from college. And this Catholic friend I just mentioned was a sorority sister. She was my friend, but my husband's friend, too, you know, as couples. You visit back and forth. I think that's inevitable, don't you? My close friends, my husband's close friends, yes this is true. Because they were his close friends before he married me, but each of them became mutually close. We married and as couples we had very good and warm relationships through the years, although originally it was my husband's friend.

In a similar vein, one woman who was married for the first time in middle age, when questioned about the effect of her marriage on her friendships, responded, "I got more friends. I got his friends, too."

Once marriage occurred, couple-oriented informants were most likely to report acquiring as friends persons with whom both they and their spouses were compatible. One man described the effects of his marriage:

> Most of the recent friends I've made have been collective, husband and wife, and their relationship has been with my wife and me. I haven't made any individual friends. Maybe that's the way, later in life, maybe that's what happens, I don't know. We have many close friends here, but they're all husband and wife.

Another man could identify only one area of his life in which he and his wife had not shared friends, including both those that they each had brought to the marriage and those acquired after:

> We shared friends. Very much so. With one exception. Some of the downtown people that I worked with on civic stuff, she didn't know them, but except for that we shared friends. I was never much for leaving my wife to go out with the boys. I mean I preferred being with her. And you see, her circle of friends were all girls that I knew, too, because we were usually together with the husbands and wives.

In a couple-oriented marriage, the husband and wife may not socialize with the same individuals, but the expectation that the marriage formed the foundation for friendships was apparent:

> My wife has been pretty active in church. She belongs to a circle, so her friends—she know the gals better than I do and I know the fellas, from the men's club.

The importance of spousal support in establishing and maintaining friendships was indicated by one woman:

> So I think by and large being aware of other people and opening up your home is the basis for friendship. And I've had that all my life and my husband was the same way. So there was never a barrier that I had to fight. My husband preferred entertaining in his home rather than going elsewhere, although he went everywhere. We belonged to the symphony and the playhouse and all that, you know, but he was very hospitable and so was his family, so that just worked out that way.

One man had had a very small number of friends in his life whom he considered special, but he was included in his wife's social activities:

All our friendships came from my wife. After she became the manager, I rode on her tail. We were invited to a lot of places, so as her husand I got into them and that's how we got into a lot of parties. But even when we were first married, we lived in a very nice, old apartment, and every Sunday—we didn't have much money at all, that was in the Depression times—but you always had enough money for a couple of bottles of gin, and we made some hors d'oeuvres; you could always have a cocktail party. We always had a lot of parties and had a lot of people up. My wife loves to entertain. We had soup and pumpernickel bread and people loved to come. So we did a lot of entertaining despite the fact that I was much more antisocial. My wife was the one who kind of pulled the social wagon around. But it paid off in the end. Those years were good. So many of our friends were really friends with my wife, these people that I'm talking about now. I'm a loner.

The people with whom he socialized he did not consider close friends, but he maintained a strong sense of obligation to them and at the time of the interview reported assisting many who were dealing with various problems associated with old age.

For at least some members of the middle class, the two symbols of individual and couple friendship orientations were golf and bridge. One man explained,

I think many men have their friends on the golf course, which I haven't had. So oftentimes that's a separate set of friends from the ones your wife has, but oftentimes the wife plays bridge and the husband plays golf. We haven't been that kind of couple. Her friends are my friends and vice versa.

They often played bridge together with other couples. Participation in leisure-time activities, then, is an important clue to whether married persons have an individual or a couple orientation to friendship.

Some of the informants, all of whom were classified as using the independent style of friendship, felt that their spouses were their best friends to the degree that others were simply excluded. Many of the acquisitive informants and some of the discerning ones also considered their spouses to be their best friends, but not to the degree of excluding all others. One informant, for example, identified a great many people whom she knew, but none whom she could describe as a close friend. She had this to say about her husband:

So we were in business together. We traveled together and we enjoyed each other's company to such a great extent we were each other's best friend. So we had a wonderful partnership. Usually the family affairs took care of most of the dates because there were so many brothers-in-law and sisters, then their children and weddings and so on, so we were greatly involved. But since we had so much of the outside world, our Saturdays and Sundays were private days. And on Wednesday the shop would close at noon and we'd have a three-hour vacation.

A man who felt that he had never had any real friends illustrated his assertion:

I wouldn't say there's anyone special that I would say, outside of the woman that I married, that I would want to go ahead and say, "Well, let's go and take a vacation, spend two or three weeks somewhere."

Informants whose lives were tied exclusively to a spouse found his or her death difficult. Couple-oriented, surviving spouses noted in some cases that they were excluded from or felt uncomfortable in couple gatherings now that they were alone; but for those whose spouses were completely central in their lives, the loss went beyond this. The informant who had been in business with her husband told the interviewer:

He is so much part of everyday living. I mean I didn't dispense with every physical thing of his. I have his Scotch scarves and I wear his Scotch wool robe, and I have many things about him. I even have some of his visor caps that I wear. And then, sometimes when I am upset and so on, he has his picture there and I talk to him. And he's part of the family thoughts and the family circles, but he's away, he's not here physically, but he's here spiritually.

She had been widowed for five years at the time of the interview. The man cited above who regarded his wife as the only person to whom he felt close enough to spend a two-week vacation explained his difficulty with being widowed:

My wife was the best woman I ever met, the best woman I ever met. I had her picture out for a long, long time. I was getting very remorseful, you know what I mean. I went to see my doctor and he asked me certain questions about my life and he asked me if I happened to have a picture of her laying around. I said, "Yes, I have." He said, "Let's try something. Why don't you just take it, wrap it up, and put it away for a while and that way you might be able to forget just a little bit and you won't think that she's always standing in your way." If I want to do something, I see her picture and I'd say, "Did you see that? God Almighty, should I do that? Should I?" And I didn't do it; it was hindering my life. It was making me feel very bad. . . . So it's only about a month now that I put her picture away, and it has changed my life to a certain extent.

The most significant change was his acquisition of a woman friend.

Expectations for and the reality of the marital bond, then, had consequences for friendships. In some cases a spouse continued to have his or her own friends after the marriage, keeping old ones and acquiring new ones who remained outside the marriage. In these marriages persons were likely to have exclusively same-gender friendships. In others, the husband and wife became a team and for prior friendships to be maintained and new friendships added, the cooperation of the spouse was required. Members of this type of couple often claimed not to have cross-gender friends while somewhat paradoxically also claiming that couples, one of whom was the other gender, were friends. In still others spouses became one another's best friend to the degree that there was no room for friendship outside the marriage. Because competing relationships simply were eliminated, these informants had no other friends. It is these spouses who, when widowed, were bereft of friendships.

This chapter has explored two attributes of individuals—age and gender—that members of friendship dyads bring to the relationship. The focus has been on their effects on friendships throughout the life cycle. Although most relationships that were considered to be friendships were between persons similar in age, the informants did bring into their oral biographies friends who were both older and younger than they. This was especially evident in their discussions of their current situations. In order to bring in everyone whom they considered important, the criterion of age similarity was often put aside. One may speculate that this would probably be the case for informants of any age who, in oral biographies focusing on friendship, might want to include older or younger persons who were significant to them. With respect to gender, acknowledging the existence of cross-gender friendships was related to marital status. First, because cross-gender relationships are considered—it would appear universally—to have sexual overtones, they are appropriate only when individuals are single, which is the case most often in adolescence and early adulthood, and in late middle age and old age. Second, once people were married, the likelihood of their having cross-gender friends depended on whether they and their spouses had separate friends, joint friends, or only one another as friends.

CHAPTER 5

FRIENDSHIPS IN OLD AGE

In this chapter the focus is on the stage in the life cycle that the informants occupied at the time of the interviews. Because the friendships described here were not recalled from the past but were ongoing, the data presented here are the most complete. Three general topics are covered. First, the relationships between various problems associated with old age and friendships are discussed. Second, the concept of "populated biography" is introduced and its significance for understanding friendships in old age is elaborated. Third, the consequences in old age of using each of the three styles of friendship are described.

Old Age as a Unique
Context for Friendship

One of the often lamented consequences of growing old is the loss of friends, which is reflected in the declining size of high school and college graduation classes, of bridge clubs and sewing circles, of local chapters of the Veterans of Foreign Wars, and of other groups—like the "Society of the Broken Dish" (Simmel, 1950: 125), in which the specific members are not (and cannot be) replaced. Meeting and talking with those friends who have survived may become increasingly difficult due to declining health and decreased mobility. To lose old friends is to lose specific others in whom the old person may have accumulated "investments of the self" (Hess, 1972:390). These are some of the "exigencies," to use Andrei Simic and Barbara Myerhoff's (1978) term, that must be specified in order to understand friendships in old age.

Throughout the interviews, informants referred to this reality of growing old. One, for example, said,

> And I belong to a sewing circle that is 50-some years old. We just have lunch. Now most of them are sick. So I have one, two, three sick friends. But, you know, we keep in touch all the time. Go over and see them. When they can come, they come.

Another said,

> We had a card club and another friend who used to pick me up. Every two weeks we had the pinochle club. But most of them have died already. [Where did you meet these people?] In the women's club, Lithuanian women's club I belonged to. And the fraternity, Lithuanian's workers association. And then I belonged to a book club, Lithuanian book club. And another fraternity. They are closed. These small fraternities have closed with the membership dying out.

About her college graduation class, one woman said, "I have two friends left. But there aren't very many people left from my class." Another informant echoed her: "There are a few I still correspond with. Some of them every couple of months. But most of the class is dead." These groups, then, because they did not or could not recruit new members, were diminished by the death of each member. In contrast, one woman reported that she had belonged to a book club for 35 years:

> I have a Great Books group that has been going for 35 years and we meet in each other's houses every two weeks. [Has the group had the same members . . .] Yes, a good many. We're adding new ones which is why we are repeating some of the works. We think the new ones ought to have the advantages of what we read in the distant past.

This informant was classified as independent and did not refer to the group members as close friends. Members of a group whose ties to one another are weak may be more willing to include newcomers and thus avoid the consequences of the "broken dish" situation.

The age cohorts to which the old belong are shrinking in size. This, of course, is the case throughout a cohort's existence, but in modern societies the size of an age cohort drops sharply only when its members reach old age (Marshall, 1980). The future of friendships characterized by "age homophily" becomes increasingly precarious as the two members reach their seventh, eighth, and ninth decades. For example, after she retired one woman spent five summers in Nova Scotia collecting material for a book on folklore. Asked about her friends there, she replied, "I made some good friends, but they are all gone now." Another explained,

> I knew two people when I came into this hotel. Both of them are dead now. That's another thing you run into with us. Our friends are going and we have to get used to the idea, and it's not easy.

One woman lamented, "I had two very nice friends here, but they both died." Speaking of his college friends, one man said,

> The friendships were very close. I don't mean with everybody, but certain people who I knew well and our friendships kept up through the years. . . . But most of the class is dead now. There are more widows than there are members of the class.

A woman described a clique to which she had belonged:

> We had our own little club, just being silly, you know. And we'd meet and use a hammer for a gavel and just act plain crazy. I still remember. And then one of the women died. One morning she died. She was fairly young. It was right on my floor. And we never met after that. We just all felt so sad about that.

One man summed up his situation succinctly: "Between death and moving to Florida—several of our very good friends have moved away—this also makes problems for friendship."

One woman in her late 80s, still living with her husband in the house into which they had moved shortly after she was married in her late teens, responded impatiently to the interviewer's repeated question about whether she had friends, "Girls that I knew, sure, but they all passed away, you know, I'm living this long." Deaths of friends who are also old, then, become a part—though not a welcome part—of the daily lives of the old, at least for those who have friends. However, even the independent informants are affected by the changing cast of characters because they associated primarily with other old people.

Another problem confronted by chronologically old friends is that they are likely to experience and be coping with physical and mental changes (Munnichs, 1964). Even granting that the stereotypes engendered by the popular press and some social scientists portray the condition of the aged as considerably more negative than it is in fact, the likelihood of experiencing sensory changes and of having chronic illnesses in old age is very high. Many of these changes limit friends' ability to communicate with one another or to spend time together. Some of the informants referred to changes in their own physical and mental abilities. One woman complained about an effusive woman whom she described as "making passes" at people: "I never liked to be touched. And the more arthritis I get, the less I like to be touched." Referring to a friend with whom her relationship had recently deteriorated, she blamed herself, at least partly:

> It's uncomfortable. You can be uncomfortable physically and then to have the mental discomfort right on top of it. . . . I'm not as patient as I used to be because so much of me hurts. And when I hurt I'm likely to get mad.

Another woman had been quite ill during the six months preceding the interview. She had belonged to the group in which the woman had died of a heart attack at a meeting. When other members wanted to resume meeting, she did not feel that she could:

> And I think it can't be now because I don't hear. I'm all right when you and I are talking, but if I try to hear anybody's conversation, I just can't enter in. And I can't see very much. And my walking, my balance is affected, and then I get this bad ear. So you can see I have a lot of things against me.

One woman had not attended the 50th reunion of her college graduation class, which also meant not getting to see her "best friend":

> I just couldn't do it. I can't hobble around campus. I have to walk very slowly. You're always walking, you know, and I can't do it. And I was so fat I didn't want anyone to see me. So I didn't go.

These women, then, spoke of their own physical problems which mitigated against their continuing to be actively involved in new friendships.

References also were made to changes in friends' behavior or capacities that interfered with maintenance of friendships. One woman spoke of a friend whom she had met each summer for the past decade at a camp that they both attended:

> And she won't be going back either. She's younger than I am, but she had a terrific sick spell, awful. She's worse off than I am.

About one of her college friends with whom she had maintained a relationship, she said,

> I think she has turned out to be a bit forgetful. If I hear from her, it's a Christmas card in March. This is what you are going to run into with us, that we are missing people that we were close to, either because they have fallen apart or dropped dead.

A more recently acquired friend who lives in the same retirement hotel also concerns her:

> And this is one of the things about friendship for older people—that our friends start slipping mentally. And we have to get used to it. And part of getting used to it is saying, "Am I getting like that, too?" It's inevitable and uncomfortable. I have a very good friend, a new friend, with whom I eat luncheon and dinner almost every day. She'll be 90 next month. She's slipping mentally. She scolded the heck out of me after lunch today because she had expected me to eat with her. And I had no idea of eating with her. That is what happens to friendship in this big upper age group.

Physical and mental changes in friends, then, affect the content of relationships.

It is likely that friends who are both old will experience physical and mental changes that interfere with their continued relationships. One woman, for example, described a friend who had recently died:

> She had been stone deaf and not seeing anyone much, and I haven't been able to get out since I don't drive. And since she's hard of hearing, I couldn't call her up. I had to relay a message and it wasn't very satisfactory.

The combination of her friend's deafness and her own lack of transportation made their interaction "unsatisfactory." She continued to think of her as a friend, however: "She's an old friend; someone I always loved dearly. I think she was a very gracious and lovely woman."

When asked if there had been any changes in her friendships since she retired, one woman described the effects of the illnesses of two of her closest friends on her relationships with them:

> The friendship certainly has been tested because our two closest friends, one has died and the other one is ill. And because it has changed the

quality in that there has been more giving on our part since the illness and the death. During the illness of the older friend and this friend who is here now, it has to be an outgoing from us because they, neither of them, is capable of giving to the other due to the illnesses they had and have. And so the quality changed in that way and it just helped to bring out the fact of how deep our friendships were. Because there was no cutting off of the friendship, that being, "You're not all right, I'm finished." That just couldn't be done. And that way, there is that little change.

These ties were evaluated as friendships, then, even though they were no longer reciprocal. In Kurth's (1970:159) words, she had developed "faithfulness" that "serves to maintain the relationship, even if the original reason for forming the relationships no longer remains."

In addition to problems presented by changes in physical and mental health, other accompaniments of old age affect relationships. One of these is widowhood. One widow, for example, explained the effects on her relationships:

> You know when you get to be a widow, men drop out of your life to an amazing degree; there just aren't enough. And couples tend to stay with couples. And I visit in the homes of couples, of course. And I invite them, but it isn't like it used to be when we were a couple. It's a very different life.

She went on to say,

> I have friends who swim, but they still have their husbands. Now you see, I don't like to join husband-wife groups. If there were single women going and they said, "Come on, let's swim," that would be a different thing. But to me, to make it a point to be over there when they go there, I wouldn't do that. I just wouldn't do it. That's all. I don't know, as a widow you walk a much more careful line in how you do things than when you were married. Life is much prettier and easier when you're a married couple. The places you go, the way you do things, the kind of invitations you give and accept.

One woman, who in her marriage used the couple orientation to friendship, was not a widow but was having some problems dealing with her husband's changed health status:

> I was a wallflower. I said that I was always happy to fall in my husband's shadow. And he's always been a real fun person. Until he became ill. He had a marvelous sense of humor.

Even before widowhood, then, couple-oriented married persons may have difficulty coping with changes in their spouses' health status.

Among other changes that affected friendships, two important ones were relative financial status and lack of transportation. The former was not referred to often, in large part because homophily dictates that friends are of the same socioeconomic status. One man, however, did cite his current financial problems as affecting his friendships:

> The first five years we were retired, it was just marvelous. We just had a wonderful time visiting around and going to Europe and so forth. But these last three years, I'd say the last three years, have not been very happy ones. And you have to try to be happy, you have to push yourself, at least I do. And I think, as I said, that most of it is financial. If I had the energy to get out and get a job . . . but I don't. I don't have energy to do it. Some people get old fast and some of them don't. I think I'm getting old fast.

Speaking specifically of his current friendships, he said,

> The problem with that at the moment is that our financial situations are farther and farther apart. They have more and more money and we have less and less. And, although our friendship remains strong, it still is not as much so, as when they say, "We want to go to Virginia Beach," or "We want to go here or there, why don't you join us?" We have to say "no" because we just can't afford it. That's the difference between public employees as I was and employees in industry, where their income doesn't decrease as much in retirement years.

Maintaining friendships with people whose incomes were significantly different from his posed problems. The feelings of friendship were strong, but the opportunities to act on feelings were limited.

Transportation, or more accurately the lack of it, presented another major obstacle. One woman explained that because she lived in the city she could get a taxi to take her to a homebound friend in a nearby suburb, but she could not get one to pick her up again. This meant that she simply was unable to visit her friend. Another described difficulties encountered in trying to meet someone with whom she was friendly:

> But we have a disadvantage because neither one of us drives and she won't take buses. If I go on the weekend I'm afraid to be alone on the bus stop waiting, because there's nobody around. There isn't as much traffic on a

weekend and every time somebody passes, you just shake. You don't know what's going to happen.

Because neither she nor the other woman drove, they had to rely on public transportation which precluded meeting at night and on weekends.

The urban area in which most of these informants lived does not have a pleasant climate, particularly in winter. It is also an area from which young people have been likely to move. After retirement, then, many people moved to warmer climes or to areas near their adult children. Those left behind often felt the loss of their friends and associates. For example, one man had friends who were "snowbirds":

> One friend of ours, we shared medical offices for a number of years. We rented a divided office. And that was a significant relationship. We're still close friends. I haven't mentioned him, as a matter of fact. He's a few years older than I am and we see him. The thing is, they're away all winter. They're away about six months out of the year. That interferes in a close friendship. When they come back we pick it up again, but it's a handicap to a friendship. There are a number of our friends who go away for the winter. We haven't because I'm working. I can only get away for a month a year; that's the vacation I get. So we can't go away the whole winter the way some of these people who are totally retired can. So that interferes with friendship in the later years. Several of them do that. So we always kid them that in winter we're here alone, which is not exactly true, but you feel abandoned.

Someone who had acquired a new best friend said,

> At one point in my life, when I retired, it was very lonely because most of my friends have left the area. . . . While volunteering does fill a need, it's not the same as a personal friendship.

Not only deaths, then, but no longer being geographically proximate affects the active continuation of friendships.

Extensive Populated Biographies

At any given point in time, individuals possess what Erving Goffman (1963:57) described as a personal identity, "the unique combination of life history items that come to be attached to the individual." Many, if not all, of these are constructed through participation in social relationships. In Andrei Simic and Barbara Myerhoff's (1978:231) words, "Aging is the result of an individual's passage through time, through the life cycle, through *a chain of interpersonal exchanges and relationships*" (emphasis added). It is these relationships that constitute the "populated biography" of an individual. Often persons' lives are presented as attributes rather than as relationships with others—for example, educational status, marital status, and occupation. Each of these attributes, however, was acquired and maintained through interaction with other people who, taken together, form the "populated biography" of any given person.

The concept of populated biography directs attention to the actual social relationships in which someone has participated, rather than to abstract characteristics of the person. For example, Jennie-Keith Ross (1977) points out the importance of actual social ties from the past when she describes the introduction of newcomers to those already in residence in Les Florales, the French retirement apartment complex she describes in *Old People, New Lives* (p. 109):

> The first day the new arrivals are clearly on display at their separate table. If someone in the community has seen one of them before, on a CNRO-sponsored vacation, or on a job, this is often the moment of recognition. Several new people told me how relieved and excited they were to see a familiar face and to hear someone say "didn't I meet you in the mountains," or "weren't you a mason for Girard and Co.?" New names also begin to circulate as the committee members talk over the morning's experience at their own tables. Sometimes a name is recognized when a face has changed or been forgotten. This kind of instant recognition triggers a move, often the next day, to a regular table with other established residents, either the person who knew the newcomer, or someone else chosen by that person.

Clearly, social relationships to which individuals have been party in the past are important in the present context. The fact that someone retired from Girard and Co. may be used by a sociologist to code socio-economic status. What is important here, however, is not an abstract job but the fact that it connects an individual to particular people, some of whom happen to be available in this setting. By allowing the populated biographies of informants to come into play, it is evident that "new lives" in new settings are related to "old lives," comprising concrete social relationships that the residents bring with them.

The old, relative to others, have longer biographies, more life history items attached to them. Holding other social variables constant, the old in modern societies are likely to have participated in more social relationships than younger others. Elapsed time since having met and befriended someone is also likely to be greater for the old than for the young. Lifelong friendships are longer, have weathered more storms successfully. For an 80-year-old, high school friends are people he or she knew initially over 60 years ago. For a 30-year-old, the elapsed time is much shorter. All things being equal, then, "more" and "longer" describe the social relationships of the old relative to the young.

Two aspects of friendships that were important in old age can be considered using the concept of populated biographies. First, in some cases informants had maintained "active" relationships with friends throughout their lives:

> When I was in elementary school, she was in my class. She had come up from Kentucky, so she joined us in the sixth grade. And we went on through school together. We were not particularly good friends because I went with one group of people and she went with another. When we got through high school, my friends went off to college and I couldn't afford it. So she and I went to summer school and got our work done in summers and taught in winters and that kind of thing. We became very close friends. And she has seen me through my blindness, which was 26 years, and is very, very good to me. I would say she's my closest, dearest friend.

Her friend, then, was an old friend in both meanings of the word. In old age these two women have been friends almost all of their lives. Another person described his first date:

> I never had a date until I was 17. My first date was with the minister's daughter. By the way, we're still buddies with her. She and her husband are—her husband died a year and a half ago—but we buddy around with her, them. He was in scouts with me, too, and that's where I met him.

Others' friendships did not go back quite so far but were nevertheless established early in the life course:

> But probably my closest friend I met in training. And we see each other very frequently. He lives very close by here. We socialize together and see each other frequently. We trained in the same hospital, so that's probably my closest friend.

One woman reported,

> I met her around 1936 and she's still a friend. We worked together. We still
> do things together. We make trips together. We met working at a hotel.
> We would always go out together. We would have trips together. We go as
> sisters, like that, you know.

Another woman described a friend to whom she had been close during
her adult life and whom because of circumstances she considered to be
her best friend at the time of the interview:

> My best friend here has been a friend of mine since the 1940s. We're social
> workers, retired. We had tickets to the symphony half series year after
> year after year, and now she lives here.

Some of the informants, then, maintained active friendships throughout
their lives with associates from childhood or early adulthood.

In other cases persons whom they had met but not considered friends
earlier in the life course were considered friends now. One woman
described her experience at an adult education program she began
attending a year before the interview:

> I met a woman that I was friendly with. Well, not a close friend, but I had
> been friendly with. She's in the same sorority I'm in. And I met her again. I
> hadn't seen her for quite a few years. I'd say she was a friendly
> acquaintance.

In singling out a fellow student, then, it was not a new acquaintance, but
an old one, that was identified. Someone else described a similar
occurrence:

> I'm pretty close now to this fella who's the vice president of this group.
> Although I've known him for 15 years, I haven't been too close to him. But
> we've been working together closely on this now. We've been in their
> home. They've been in our home. I just knew him casually from church.

One woman described someone whom she did not really consider a
friend, although there is a very good chance that she may attain that
status in the future. The informant had planned to move to Florida with
this woman's sister:

We never were that close, but we still keep in touch. I was closer to her sister that passed away. That was one of my friends that I went to school with from kindergarten up. She was the bratty sister of my friend. She always calls me when she's depressed because she says I cheer her up.

Another woman described her most recently acquired friends:

This woman had a daughter my son's age and they were in the choir together, so we worked on this thing for the choir, fund raising, the things you do. This was years back. And then my daughter got into school, and this woman turned out to be her third or fourth grade teacher. So I had that contact with her, and we happened to run into them over at a play in the park one night. And so they said, "Well, let's get together," and, "Do you play bridge?" And now we have a real good friendship with them. Now we see them every two or three weeks. We get together and play bridge with them and we go to plays with them. And we enjoy each other very, very much.

In many cases, then, for these old informants it was not meeting strangers but persons already known that led to friendships—reacquaintance rather than new acquaintance. As each person moves through life, accumulating an increasing number of social relationships, he or she is also collecting resources in the form of people who may be drawn upon later in life.

Many of the informants had lived in the same area all of their lives. They were very likely, then, also to be surrounded by many people whom they had known for a great many years, and there were references to this sprinkled through their conversations with the interviewers. One woman, for example, described one of her first social forays after her retirement:

While I was at this meeting, I realized that there were many people that I did know, people that I went to school with. . . . It's good to know that you can go out and see a familiar face.

A man described his first few days in a retirement community located in the same town in which he had lived since early adulthood:

I found that the people were just delightful. The first few days I went in and ate alone, but people would stop off at the table, and then some of them remembered back to when I was active in civic stuff in the community.

Someone else reported a similar feeling of belonging to the community. She had lived in the same house since she was ten, but preferred meeting people with whom she had worked through the years:

> I like friends that I used to have at work because they're people that I used to go out to lunch with. We talked about the same things—about the same bosses, the same people we worked with, the same material we handled— so I like to meet them. Of course, not too many of them are working any more. Most of them gave up long before I did. . . . Those are the people I like best. We kind of speak the same language. And then we hear from old bosses that have retired and moved out of town. And they'll tell me what this one said and I'll have some letters from somebody. We meet in downtown restaurants in the daytime. We're afraid at night. We probably tell 20 people, and maybe 12 come.

Although the community with which she identified was not defined by territorial boundaries, she helped to arrange to bring its members together periodically. Another woman, because of the business that she and her husband operated, belonged to organizations and had contacts with many people in the community where she continued to reside after the death of her husband. Some informants returned to the communities after living someplace else for a number of years, not because of specific friends but because of the niche they held in the community. For example, one man had returned to a city after living several years in another one. He had held a prestigious position and felt that he would be able to reestablish relationships:

> It's not been a question of making a lot of new friends. It's sorting out the old ones. Some of them you just try to recognize when you see them at parties, and others you find you're fairly close to.

Another man, a retired minister, also found a place in the church in which he and his wife had grown up and married. Although they had no close friends in the congregation, they were well known and had no trouble establishing ties when they returned.

Long-time friends were not always considered the ideal by those who had them. For example, one informant reported of her childhood friends:

If I haven't seen them for two or three years, we can just pick up where we left off. But I've found that after a week, I get sort of impatient with them. We haven't had the same experiences. After we've talked about their grandchildren and things, we run out of things to say.

Another woman, who lived in the same retirement community as an old friend, also found that spending time with her was increasingly trying:

You also find that living under the same roof with someone you have known for years may turn out to be hazardous. Someone who lives here—she and I worked for the same social agency for several years. I think she has had a personality change. Maybe I have. She's a talker and nothing stops her talking. I'm a talker. I can stop. But she is such a talker that she has turned people off. They don't want to bother. It's too bad. She is very helpful to a lot of people. It makes me sad. It makes me very sad that she bores me spitless.

A man who would have understood her ambivalent feelings said,

I really don't think that lifelong friends are all that good. In fact, I'd just as soon chuck the lot of them. In fact, I'd just as soon make new friends to beat the band. If we just get together, Saturday night, conversation is apt to be, well, I suppose there's some quiet amusement because of all the things we've known over the past 60 or 65 years of mutual friendship, but there's also a big liability to old friends because you gotta accommodate the sons of bitches and their rotten personalities. . . . At least with new friends you can select them.

Thus old friends are not always considered to be a blessing. People do change through the courses of their lives, and in old age they may have little positive feeling other than a sense of obligation with respect to friends made earlier in life.

In describing their most recently acquired friends, populated biographies played another important role. Quite often, others known to the informant—friends, acquaintances, or relatives—were important in providing the link to the new friend. In some cases the tie to the mediating person was "weak," in other cases "strong" (Granovetter, 1973). For example, one person identified her most recently acquired friend as a woman whose children had been students of her best friend and roommate. She and her best friend lived in a retirement community and when this woman moved in, "she came to see my roommate because

she knew her children. And she's with us about 90% of the time."
Another woman described someone she had met at a senior citizens
center:

> She happened to sit at my table one day and she told me her last name.
> And then, as she was leaving, I said I was glad to know her and I hoped
> she'd come back again. And she said, "How could you remember my
> name?" and I said, "When I used to go to Erie on vacation, there were
> people next door by that very same last name." And she says, "Well, you
> know, my husband was from Erie." But of course he died, and she said, "I
> don't know if they are relatives or not." She likes to go to Value City. And
> she lives alone. And she's very nice. I'm glad I met her there.

One woman said that she had attended a meeting with a woman she had
known "for a long time but we had never really developed a friendship."
At the meeting, however,

> This person introduced me to a very lovely woman whom I had never seen
> before, and it seemed as though she sought me out. Well, I could feel that I
> would like to develop a friendship with her.

At the time of the interview she regarded this new friend as her best
friend. One man, when asked if he had made any friends more recently
than those already mentioned, replied,

> Yes, we've made some friends in the last five years or so, some new friends
> that we see fairly often. One couple in particular that we see two or three
> times a month go out to dinner together and so forth. We met them
> through other friends. The friends that I told you moved to Florida, who
> we're very close to yet, they were friends of theirs. We met through them.

One woman who lived in a retirement community described her most
recent friend, her meal companion. The interviewer asked how she
happened to strike up an acquaintance with her:

> My sister-in-law wrote to me and told me to look her up and gave me a
> background of her work as a volunteer in a hospital and the college and
> sorority business. That meant I had to get busy.

Another source of ties to likely candidates was described by someone
else:

And then there is another man who went to my college who is 10 or 15 years younger than I am who is a very close friend. He used to come in every week up at the house, and then we'd sit down and have a drink and chin together. He's a wonderful friend. He's one of the very close ones.

In this case the local alumni association was important. His eating companion in his retirement community was acquired through one of his wife's best friends:

I now eat breakfast every day with this friend of hers. We have become almost like two brothers. And we now eat dinner together, too, which is great.

In all likelihood, acquiring friends through "weak ties" is typical of the acquisitive throughout the life span. However, since very few informants could remember the circumstances under which they met their friends, only more recently acquired ones were remembered as initially mediated through others. The independent informants, who were not seeking friends, and the discerning, who had only strong ties, were not as open to acquiring friends through other people.

Friendship Styles in Old Age: Biography and Circumstance

Recognition that the old have extensive biographies often clouds the fact that they, like younger social actors, continue to be governed by the "pragmatic motive"—that is, their "attention to this world is primarily determined by what [they are] doing, have done or plan to do in it" (Berger and Luckmann, 1967:22). Examining friendships by focusing only on biography and ignoring the present circumstances with which an old person is faced would therefore give an incomplete picture. With respect to friendship, how do biography and circumstance interact in old age? The styles of friendship into which the informants were sorted had a clear relationship to their friendship patterns in old age. Hence, each style is addressed in turn.

CIRCUMSTANCE: THE INDEPENDENTS

In old age the independents continued to be affected primarily by the circumstances that surrounded them. Since their friendships were more accurately characterized as friendly relations—less personal relationships than those of either the discerning or the acquisitive—their participation in social relationships was dependent on the particular "pool" in which they happened to be. One informant who lived in a retirement community referred to only one woman there whom she considered a friend. She was not isolated, however:

> I'm involved in a good many activities here. I've always been a people person. I figure when there is something going on at the museum, somebody from here should go on over there. So I call up and make arrangements for transportation and get them over there. We're going to the Shakespeare festival next week.

Later in the interview she said,

> I'm not musical, but I've been going to the symphony with a group of people. I always have somebody that I go with and we have our season tickets. And there's a common interest that brings us together and makes us continue to see each other.

She was willing, then, to be a friend of "somebody" with whom she shared an interest and, as her reference to music indicated, she was willing to adopt an interest, if necessary. The more general nature of her biography, however, was important to her current social relationships. She had always been single and had taught school until she retired at age 70:

> My people experience is different than that of the women that have had families and family responsibilities, family joys, and family worries. So that is something. I don't have any close friends here that are family people. I think my inclination . . . is to gravitate towards people who have been professional people rather than family people.

It was not particular social relationships but the more general course of her life that was significant to her current relationships. The only problem that might arise for her would be living in a place where there were no people with whom she shared a common interest, but given her willingness to adapt, this seemed unlikely.

Others who were classified as independent relied on their environment to provide them with friendly relations. One man, for example, said the following about his current friends:

I got a lot of friends, too, but I don't say they're friends that I would depend upon. They're friends that talk to me, friends that I like to talk to, but I would never put myself in the position where I'd have to say, "Well, I need this. Can you help me with this?" Friends are friends, are good people to talk to. That's about all you can expect, especially today. Today it's dog eat dog.

In the course of the interview, he described his relationship with a man in the retirement apartment complex where he lived:

I have one man in this building today—he's about 84 years of age—we have become quite friendly. And he has a lady friend, too. And we both have gardens. And someone stole his car from here about six months ago, so I've been riding him around with his girlfriend and, well, we have a few drinks together, too. He's about the closest one, I would really say so, in my life. He's about the closest one because I've been alone all this while [his wife died three years ago]. We talk to each other on the telephone practically every day. He'll call me up. . . . He came after I did. He lost his wife about five years ago. She died. He's a heavy set man. I would say that we respect one another. We don't go out together or anything like that, but everybody knows that him and I are pretty thick when it comes to living in this building here. Everybody knows that. Because for a long time I had to use a cane on account of my leg and he was using a cane. And we used to go to the cafeteria next door to have a couple of sandwiches and they used to call us the Golddust Twins because we both had red caps and we both had canes and we'd hobble along the street. We did that for quite a long time. Him and I get along pretty good.

Even though outward appearances indicated to others that a friendship existed—everybody "knows" that the two men are "pretty thick"—in this informant's own mind, this man was only someone with whom to spend time, not a real friend.

Another independent informant flourished on friendly relationships and organized her daily life so that she would come in contact with many people:

I appreciate people in groups. I like lectures and all that, saying "hello" to people that I know, but not to ask them over because that means staying home. . . . I never say to anybody, "Why don't you come over and visit me?" Never. Because I like to be on the go. Now a lot of the tenants where I live have asked me to come over and visit them, but I'd feel confined just as though I was in my own apartment. In order to be actively living, I feel you've got to mix, you've got to be out where the crowds are. Now at my age so many people don't like noise and the crowds, but I just love it.

One man had a prepared speech about how to make friends and why it was important to have them, although by friends he meant "friendly relations":

If you have a feeling of uselessness, if nobody needs or wants you, you ought to do something about it. So the question asked is just what to do. As a starter, change your habitual way of thinking, acting, and feeling. And decide to do the following: Well, okay, let's say, play cards, dancing, join some social clubs, go to some lectures and some concerts, things like that. Then you'll have something to talk about with people. . . . As long as a person continues to force himself into social relationships with other human beings, not in a passive way but as an active contributor, he will gradually find that most people are friendly and that he is accepted. As shyness and timidity begin to disappear, he feels more comfortable in the presence of others, other people, and with himself.

In the discussion with the interviewer following his opening speech, he explained that he followed his own advice:

Oh I had quite a time of it, to tell the truth. Myself, it's more or less as I said in my paper, that I force myself to do it. And I still do. I found I was getting into quite a rut. I more or less didn't want to associate with people anymore. I broke away. And I thought, "This cannot go on." So occasionally what I do, I'm really not allowed to eat at the other Center because I don't live there, but I do go there. And I like that group very much and I make it a point to sit at different tables so I can meet people. And they have some dances.

This man, whose wife died shortly before he retired, found himself living alone in an apartment with little access to other people. Dissatisfied with his isolation, he forced himself to meet people, although—consistent with his style of friendship—his goal was simply being around other people rather than establishing close ties.

Another man also had found the senior citizens center near his home useful:

I like it. I mean the people are nice. What has helped me a lot, too, is that I might see people that are blind and people here that. . . . Now today they had some come in from that nursing home. They come in every Monday. Ones in wheelchairs, ones with walkers. Now look at them. If I'm feeling sorry for myself in the morning when I get up, I've found the best cure that I have for that is when I come in and see people that are worse off than I am. And then always I forget that I'm feeling sorry for myself. Because I consider myself very fortunate that I can get around.

One woman who lived in a retirement community described her living situation:

This is a wonderful place for an older person if they're an outgoing person which I think I am. Everybody is your family and you visit them and find out about them and you find interests, you see, that you share, and then you add them to your circle.

Again, it is not establishing close friendships, but being around other people that is important to her.

One woman, who received a telephone call during the interview, might not have included the caller in her discussions:

Oh, I can tell you about the one that called me. I just met her at a bus stop one day about two years ago. We just picked up a conversation. She lives just over here. She's an artist and I kind of like her. She's a nice person. She calls me quite often and I call her and we meet often. [To do things?] Well, we don't do much of anything. [Just talk?] Yeah, be with somebody, eat out or something like that, you know. We don't tell our problems or anything like that, but, you know, if a person doesn't feel well, you like to know someone's concerned or you talk about it and that helps. She's kind of a delightful person. [You just met her at a bus stop?] Yeah. I meet a lot of people. I talk to everybody and I find them very interesting, you know. You'd be surprised. You run into people that other people never had a chance to meet. And she's just nice to be with. There are some people you could know and be with and you might just as well not be with anybody. And I'd rather be alone than be bothered with someone that I find annoying. I mean I don't want to be so desperate that I just have to put up with anything.

All of these independent informants relied on their living situations to provide people with whom to talk or pass the time. They were not interested in establishing close ties. Their expectations, then, were relatively easily satisfied. It is probably not surprising that many of them lived in retirement housing and that the others spent time at senior centers. These age-homogeneous settings provide others with whom it is relatively easy to be friendly without being personally committed.

The one informant for whom a lifetime of friendly relations proved troublesome was a single woman who had spent her childhood in an orphanage. Although her brother was still living, they were not close and he lived 2000 miles away. She had no close relatives. Unlike other informants who shared these characteristics but were classified as acquisitive, she had no one on whom to depend when she encountered problems When the interviewer inquired, she replied,

> Well, yeah, but maybe I don't want to have to count on them. Maybe they would, but I don't want to. Like I have to have surgery on my feet. I have real bad feet. I've been putting it off because I worry about the postoperative care. I'd have to have a foot cast for six weeks and then there's a six month healing period. And you know, my feet are my security. And sometimes you really realize, I mean, who can you really call on? I mean, you don't want to impose on anybody really, but it's pretty hard if you're more or less alone with no family ties or something. I have cousins and all that, but when your life is so different you just don't have much in common. . . . Yeah, sometimes I think about how there are days when nobody knows whether you're alive or dead. My cousin might call me every other week and I could die in between.

This woman, living by herself in an apartment, faced troublesome problems in old age when her health status threatened to deteriorate seriously.

BIOGRAPHY: THE DISCERNING

Informants who were classified as discerning were least affected by the current circumstances of their lives with respect to whom their friends were but the most vulnerable to their friends no longer being available. Loss of these friends means that they will become friendless, and unlike the independents for whom lack of friends was only rarely presented as a problem, some of these old people were likely to be very lonely.

One women, for example, found very painful the period of her life when her two friends were not available to her. The loneliness she felt during her 20s and early 30s when she lived in New Hampshire and Buffalo was evident in her voice as she recounted her experiences. Throughout the years she relied on her husband as an important source of friendship:

My husband is the kind of person who is a real friend. I mean, he's the kind of person who loves to talk, and he made up for all of that sort of thing [loneliness]. He has, sort of, all through the years, been a real friend, very companionable. . . . I think that that's one reason that I haven't really had to seek out friends very much, because we're together an awful lot and on a really friendly basis.

At the end of the interview, when she and the interviewer were tying up loose ends, she said,

Wait a minute, I just thought of one other very good friend—my daughter. My daughter moved back to town recently and lives quite close. I really consider that we have a friendship. She's a great person.

She went on to explain that her daughter, who was married and had two children, recently had moved back to town and started graduate school. One of the things the informant had missed in friendships was someone "whose mind matched mine," someone who was willing to discuss books and ideas that interested her. Now she had her daughter. She was relatively young, only 68, but if the remaining years of her life are continuous with her past, her friendships are very likely to dwindle to the one with her daughter—the only relationship remaining in her biography that she will call a friend.

One man whose "true close friend" was living, but not in the same town as he, described his feelings of "desolation" (Townsend, 1957):

I think that one of the areas for a person who's living alone, what you might call the aged group—you can keep yourself busy. I keep myself busy. I'm out quite a few times at night. But when you are back by yourself, there's a lonesomeness that just isn't satisfied with the casual meetings of friends. I don't know what it is.

As he indicated, he was not isolated:

One of the things, I say, I'm fortunate to have the club avenues. If I didn't have those, I wonder how I would fare actually.

But his relationships with the men in these clubs does not satisfy his yearning for a close relationship:

I can point to people that I know in the clubs. I see them frequently, so that when you do meet, whether you like them or not, you converse, you act and react. And the fact that you see each other frequently—let's say you come up to some point where there is a need on the part of one party or the other—there might be some contact there, where the one person will respond to the need of the other. Whether you turn to them consciously or unconsciously. Lots of people don't like to turn to anyone. I find it difficult, but if I get into trouble I don't know who I'd call.

After some thought he decided that he would contact his daughter in New York first and then call the widow of a fraternity brother with whom he had established a friendship after their respective spouses had died. As he stated, "most of what I call friends are of pretty long standing. I haven't made any friends of that degree recently." He was vulnerable in old age, then, because his style of friendship left him feeling bereft. The loneliness he felt he attributed to being male:

Over the course of the last ten years, since I've been widowed, I've come to observe that men who become widowed do not seem to be able to join together easily and maybe provide the daily contact, like the widows do. Now these gals I know, widows, are in constant contact with other widows all the time, calling each other, doing things together. Men don't do that; at least I haven't experienced it.

More accurately, the discerning do not experience it. The acquisitive and independent informants, expecting less from relationships, were more likely to be in contact with others and to find those contacts satisfactory.

Another man whose only friends generally were people whom he had known before immigrating to the United States, speculated about the probable effects of his wife's death on his friendships:

I do not think it would have any effect with these people in New York and these people in California. If my wife would go before me, I would definitely drop completely out of the scene here. [Even with the one man that you met recently?] Yes. Maybe I would see him once in a great while, have lunch together in a restaurant, but that would be all. Because these people in town I only keep the semblance of friendship, only because of my wife. These people have nothing to tell me, to say to me, and I have nothing to say to them.

In all likelihood, then, this discerning informant will become completely isolated if he outlives his wife. He defines his current, local relationships as a waste of his time. His two close friends are not geographically proximate, and one of these will probably die of cancer soon.

Another man who was classified as discerning planned to maintain relationships with his wife's friends if she were to die before him. He had had only a few close friends during the course of his life, although none was alive at the time of the interview, but he liked to be around people:

> I have to say that so many of our friends were generated or they were really friends with my wife. These people that I'm talking about now, these old friends. I would not go out and seek friends. As I say, I'm a loner and I have a great many interests of my own. As I say, I go down to school to take courses and I really don't need a great deal of friendship. Now, don't misunderstand me. You always like to have a few people. As you know, as you get older, there isn't anything worse, even if you're young, than to eat alone. . . . Of course, I like a few friends and I have a few friends. And if anything happened to my wife, I would still have a few friends. I would still have people for dinner because I'm a good cook. I believe in that. See, I believe that as you get older, the one way to hold friends is not to become inactive but to continue to invite people up. . . . Many people get lazy, you know. They want that sort of social life, but they don't want to do a damn thing to promote it or to activate it themselves.

Compared with the previous informant, whose wife also was responsible for promoting relationships, this man had very different expectations about how widowhood would change his life.

Other discerning informants at some point in their lives had "matured" and were no longer seeking intense friendships. In essence, they became more like the independents, associating with people in friendly relations and not expecting anything deeper to develop. One man who had had two friends—one deceased and the other lost in a move—described his situation at the time of the interview:

> My closest friends at this point in time have all passed away, the ones I was really close to, and that's just in the last three or four years. And even some of those I lost more or less contact with in the last, oh, ten years. We'd see each other just occasionally. They were the closest friends I had. . . . Now the friends that I've made in the recent, oh, like the last 10 to 15 years, were either through people that I worked with or just came in contact with on the outside. And there weren't any real close friendships. . . . But the only people now that I consider, that I'm still in contact with—and that's just to see on occasion, I don't have any close friends—are some of these people that I worked with or worked for, and some of them are still working.

When asked if there had been times in his life when he felt that having friends was more important than at other times, he said,

> Well, I think just due to the fact of inactivity in these later years—that is, I'm not as active as I was at one time—and I think my friends were more important to me when, my close friends, going back so many years when I was more active and in business, socially and outside. They were a very important part of my life, yes, they would be. But now in these later years, in the last ten years or so, or say the last five years—it's not that I'm secluded and getting tired out, that sort of thing—but the people that I was close to, as I've said, I lost contact with, so that gradually that sort of fades into the past. And it's not that I'm not conscious of their friendship. I think of them occasionally, of course, and we all have some things that come back to us, memories of enjoyable times we've had, we have certain pictures; but there isn't anything at present in the last five years or so that I could say that I've been that close.

Asked who his most recently acquired friend was, he replied,

> Well, there really isn't. I don't know. I couldn't really say. There isn't anyone really that is, you know, a close friend, that you'd care to sit down and have any personal discussions with.

Unlike other discerning informants, however, this man did not feel desolate:

> I think in the earlier years my friends were more important and took a more important place in my life than later years.

He was living in a retirement community so that he had access to other men with whom he had friendly relations. About his living situation, he said, "I like it, in general, and I'm pleasant and try to be kind and decent to everyone." This man was ever single but had helped to support his sister and her two daughters. His sister and one of his nieces lived in the area and he did not feel that there would be no one to call if an emergency arose.

Another man who had only had close friends in adolescence, when asked to identify his best current friend, responded,

> I try to be compassionate, I try to have concern, I try to be just to all the people with whom I am acquainted. And so far as selecting one

individual, my wife would be it. And yet, we never feel alone, either one of us, because we can always call on someone who we know will, if not be willing or able to help us at the moment, can give us some advice or can give us the kind of feeling that we're not alone.

After retirement, he had made a point of attending club meetings and volunteering in an area where his skills were useful and, at the time of the interview, had a very busy schedule:

Both my wife and I are active in a number of geriatric groups. I've just completed a seven-year tour of presidency of the one at our church. And I belong to the Senior Masons group up here. I belong to one at the church right up here and to one at another church. We belong to AARP and well, if you look at our calendar, you wonder how in the world we get time to do anything except attend. Well, we have to be selective so that we don't wear ourselves out, so we attend as many as we possibly can. I have spent nine years at the school up here teaching children in reading. . . . See, our philosophy is that sitting and doing nothing is the best way to go downhill rapidly in the geriatrics field. You just lose continuously, so we keep active. We take care of all the plantings along the building here, that center thing out there, and over there, do you see those pink geraniums over there? We do all that.

Later in the interview, referring again to the gardening, he said,

I don't know if we're going to do it next year or not because we have some physiological problems with both of us. My wife has had cancer, but she's had nine years of no return and that's remarkable. She has a lot of side effects, so that's one thing. Then, this last year, I had 34 radiation therapy treatments for prostate cancer. So we live from day to day and let it go at that. Do the best you can while we're doing it.

This man and his wife, then, continue in old age to be involved with other people, to participate in friendly relations with those they see at various meetings. His wife, however, is now his best friend. About other relationships he said,

I really don't believe that I have any individual without whom I couldn't live. I don't have that. I like to be friendly and respectful to all people.

When asked if he had ever had to make a choice between two friends, he replied,

Not in my case, no, and I think that is due to, largely, being selective in how you're going to be with people. If you have a plateau of how you're going to deal with people, then you don't have these ups and downs. We have some friends who make a friendship, and about two months later, they're at odds, these people are at odds. We have never, neither my wife nor I, have ever encountered anything like that so far as our relationships with nonfamily members. You may occasionally have it with family members, but not with nonfamily members. We treat everyone with courtesy and consideration. We don't go about this picking-and-choosing business. I think if a person likes you and you like a person, that will blossom one way or another into a lasting acquaintanceship or a deep-seated friendship.

In adulthood, then, this once-discerning informant adopted the style of the independents and organized his life so that he was in contact with others—again, especially others who were members of his own age cohort.

BIOGRAPHY AND CIRCUMSTANCE: THE ACQUISITIVE

For those informants who were classified as acquisitive, both biography and circumstance contributed to friendships in old age. They were likely to have friends from the past, as was evident in previous descriptions, and to be open to new ones as well. The new friendships arose out of the situations with which they were confronted in this period of their lives. Many of them were described in the preceding section of this chapter, for it is they whose populated biographies provided likely candidates for friends and who were able to use old friends as links to new ones.

One of the questions included in the interview guide was, "Who was the last [most recent] friend that you made?" Answers to this question often revealed the circumstances that called for establishing new friends. Those who lived in retirement communities that included communal dining spoke of the people with whom they ate. One woman, for example, responded to the query about her most recently acquired friend by saying,

I think it's the person I eat with every day. You mean a real friend. . . . I know that she fills a need of mine, and I know that I fill a need of hers. And we eat luncheon together practically every day and most dinners. . . . And it does beautifully for meals. It comes in very handy. "Are you tied up for dinner tonight?" "Well, yes, I'm sorry, I am." Tied up with her. And if we do want to eat with someone else, we just tell the other one, "Gee, I'm sorry. I've got to eat with so-and-so tonight." Works out nicely.

Another resident of a retirement community identified a similar impetus for acquiring a new friend:

> I know who my closest friend is now, and that's this man whom I met here . . . even though I haven't known him nearly as long as some of the others. I now eat breakfast every day with him. We have become like two brothers. And we now eat dinner together, too, which is great. What I don't particularly want to do is get involved in a series of cocktail parties. I'd rather be with someone that I am very fond of. I've kept out of it and my friend has helped me a lot because my natural tendency is to say "yes."

These new friendships were acquired, at least in part, to deal with the circumstances of the residential setting that presented these informants with situations requiring "protection" at meal times.

One widow still had close friends who lived near her, one couple in particular who included her in many of their activities. When asked to identify her most recently acquired friend, she said,

> This is a woman I had met as a result of friendships with some of the other people. She's a widow also, and we have been at different meetings together and at different friends' functions where we would be thrown together. And because we have common interests in travel and in theater, we have common interests in reading. . . . That friendship, I would say, would be of about five-years duration. It is not as complete as the others, but I find it very pleasant and we enjoy doing things together. And because of the fact that both of us are widows it makes it much easier.

Although this recent friendship was a comparatively less "complete" one, it was enjoyable, nevertheless, and was rooted, in part, in a change in circumstances—her becoming widowed.

Another woman mentioned a person with whom she shared outings. Asked if she considered her to be a friend, she replied,

> Oh, yes. I met her the first day that I went down there [senior center]. I quit work the first of May last year and I thought, "I'm not going to stay in bed and I'm not going to get lazy." So I went right down to the Senior Center on the second. And I said I was going to inquire because I wasn't going to get in a rut. . . . So, yes, she calls me up, even when her son came

from Chicago. I was the first one he called, you see, because I give the mother such confidence and he is just so glad I'm her friend.

In the course of the interview, she also described two other friends from the senior center with whom she participated in various noncenter activities. Her response to her change in circumstances—retiring—was to begin immediately to find new activities and new friends, not to replace but to supplement those she had had at her place of employment. In old age, then, the acquisitive informants drew on ties maintained from earlier in life, if possible, but also were open to new friendships when confronted with changes in circumstance for which the old ties were inadequate.

The focus of this chapter has been the current situations of the informants. In contrast to earlier periods in the life course, this last stage presents different constraints to establishing and maintaining friendships. With this stage, moreover, it is easiest to see the value of conceptualizing an individual's life as a "populated biography" and the consequences of using each of the styles of friendship. Although old age has been the vehicle for the ideas presented here, the process of friendship acquisition in other stages of the life cycle is revealed as well. Populated biographies and the important place that friendship style holds in mediating individuals' relationships with other people characterize the life cycle more generally. With respect to understanding the process of friendship, a topic that the informants had difficulty reconstructing, these data expose the ways in which individuals acquire friends and the reasons they bother to do so.

CHAPTER 6

BIOGRAPHY AND FRIENDSHIP

Beginning with a curiosity about patterns of friendship through the life course, the research project of which this book is a product was structured to allow old people to tell about their friendships in conjunction with relating their life stories. Although it was acknowledged at the outset that the word "friend" has no universal cultural meaning, informants were nevertheless encouraged to use the term as they would in everyday conversation, to talk about both their own friends and friendship in general. A number of significant features of friendship were identified inductively from analysis of the guided conversations. Before proceeding to a discussion of the broader implications of the analysis of these topical oral biographies, a brief summary is in order.

Three ways of "doing friendship" (Lofland, 1976) were described in Chapter 2. The differences among the independent, the discerning, and the acquisitive styles of friendship show that there clearly is more than one way to organize nonkin relationships through the life course. Furthermore, in Chapter 5 the cumulative consequences in old age of using each friendship style were described. Each one gave those who used it quite different social resources in old age. Dorothy Jerrome (1981:193) reports that, when older women are widowed or retire, they "compensate for the loss of close ties and the increase in leisure" in a variety of ways:

> Some women extend and deepen existing relationships. Some grow closer to siblings and cousins. Some become full-time "good neighbours" or assume responsibility for elderly relatives. Some acquire altogether new friends through voluntary associations and related social functions, or by moving into a new neighborhood.

Availability of information about someone's friendship style would provide important clues to the alternative an individual is likely to choose. Those who use the independent style, for example, cannot decide to "extend and deepen existing relationships," and the discerning are unlikely to "acquire altogether new friends."

Patterns of friendship through the life course were identified in Chapter 3. Both the maintenance of long-term relationships and the termination of friendships were discussed. It was clear that "turnings" affected initiation, maintenance, and termination of friendships, although not all informants were affected equally, with the primary mediator being friendship style. In addition, focusing on individuals' actual relationships, rather than on abstract events, revealed that for some, nonkin relationships are continuous throughout the life cycle. It was also evident that, even though there is a general belief that Americans have only short-term, superficial ties with friends, there are in fact structural supports for the maintenance of long-term, nonkin ties—for example, "home towns" and alumni groups. In Chapter 5 this topic was broached again when the concept of "populated biographies" was introduced to show that it is not abstract but concrete others that, at least for some, are important to friendships in old age.

In Chapter 4, cross-gender and age-discrepant friendships were examined. Most of the friends identified by the informants were persons of similar age and the same gender. In their middle eyars, age discrepancies existed but were not considered significant. However, some did describe relationships with persons who were different ages than they, especially at the two ends of the life course. Only when informants began to outlive their friends or their friends' health status changed did the discrepancy become difficult to ignore. Almost all of the informants agreed that there are rules governing cross-gender friendships: They should occur only when individuals are eligible for marriage. In essence, this means that the informants had cross-gender friendships in adolescence and early adulthood before they married and again later in life when they were single. Unlike same-gender friendships, long-term, cross-gender ones were uncommon, although there existed the possibility of reactivating them when persons became widowed. Somewhat paradoxically, married informants who used a couple orientation to friendships, and who therefore described members of the couple as friends, rarely described only the different-gender member of the couple as a friend.

Most of the material covered in Chapter 5 has already been described above because of its logical connection with issues raised earlier in the book. The exception is the specific problems that confront the old—the acceleration of deaths among members of the age cohort, changes in health status, transportation problems, and changes in relative income—that affect the continuation and initiation of friendships at this last stage of the life cycle. Again, the possibility of replacing lost friends was affected by friendship style.

The material presented here is a testament to the difficulty of focusing on the old without becoming sensitized to the significance of time. Sally Falk Moore (1978:24) writes, "The old themselves epitomize its passage. A description of the structure of their society now, at this moment, does not suffice to describe their experience or place. Thus, only a framework of analysis that focuses on things that happen *over time* can give a full sense of the meaning of their present." Other scholars are in agreement. Leopold Rosenmayr (1981:34), for example, writes:

> To find the basic problems of elderly people for whom social help is relevant, it is much more necessary to identify the path of their life history through a biographical reconstruction and in this art and manner to uncover their present problems and "concerns" that these life histories have generated. One cannot even recognize priorities of needs except through a life history.

This recognition is one of the major contributions of the age-stratification perspective in which it is made clear that characteristics of a given age cohort are likely to be different from both the one that proceeded it and the one that comes after (Riley, 1976, 1985).

An increasing amount of research not only on the old but on younger members of society as well is examining lives through time, recognizing not only that the historical periods in which people move through the life course are important but also that earlier events in persons' lives affect later ones (Bertaux and Kohli, 1984; Elder, 1984). This research on friendship throughout life is envisioned as adding to this body of research. Focusing on a noninstitutionalized relationship rather than the more traditional areas of work and family uncovers the consequential choices that people make in an area of their lives for which rules are absent or at least not widely shared. Arlene Skolnick (1983:386) writes:

> The life course is represented as a socially determined trajectory through time, shaped by age norms, economic constraints, institutionalized patterns. The very word "transition" suggests an impersonal, agentless movement. It is true that the life course is socially and biologically

conditioned, but it is also self-created. People make choices among the options open to them, however limited these may be.

Apparently, friendships are only minimally conditioned socially or biologically and depend much more on the agency of the social actor, the self. They clearly show the variety of experiences accumulated through time that differentiate individuals from one another and the importance of considering life stories if current situations are to be understood.

In the first chapter of the book, three frameworks within which to approach analysis of the topical oral biographies were identified. These then were employed alone or together throughout the subsequent chapters to elucidate various aspects of friendship. In this chapter each of the perspectives—social-psychological, life-course, and cultural—is used to summarize and to put into broader context the material presented in the preceding pages.

Friendship Style and the Self

Three styles of friendship—independent, discerning, and acquisitive—were introduced in the second chapter and continued to be important for understanding the lives of the informants. Although not internally consistent in all respects, the styles are distinctly different from one another. In establishing and maintaining friendships, informants clearly were affected by circumstances over which they had no control—for example, deaths ("I had two very good friends here, but they both died.") and choices made for them in childhood by parents ("My mother put an end to that!"). However, once they reached adulthood, decisions about whether to establish and maintain ties were their own, based on the importance to them of particular others (Matthews, 1983). From a social-psychological perspective, then, a significant dimension of the friendship styles is whether long-term relationships are included.

Donald Redfoot and Kurt Back (1984:4), in "The Perceptual Presence of the Life Course," suggest that "experiences of the life course are not universal, but may be classified into types that are socially distributed." In their imaginative research on the meaning assigned to objects that older women "breaking up housekeeping" chose to take with them when moving to tiny apartments, they discovered variation in meaning that was related to social class. For members of the middle class, biographical meaning was associated with chosen objects, but for those classified as members of the working and lower classes, more often immediate needs and activities were given as reasons for choosing objects. This bears a strong resemblance to the distinctions among styles of friendship. They suggest that their research

> should give pause to those who suggest the universal experience of the life course whether as a "life review" or in any other distinct form. At the very least, we should not take such experiences as universal but as empirical problems that demand that we note: 1) the degree to which the life course is a relevant experience, 2) the ways in which it is experienced by different types of people, and 3) how different types of circumstances result in different kinds of outcomes. Even if a "life review" of some sort is universal . . . we are faced with a wide range of ways in which it is manifested in the actual experiences of individuals [p. 17].

This research on friendships supports their assertion that "the perceptual presence of the life course" or, in words more consistent with the material presented here, the meaning assigned to "populated biographies" is not constant across individuals.

Using as an indicator the maintenance of long-term friendships, it is evident that populated biography was not relevant in the same way to the independent as it was to either the discerning or most of the acquisitive informants. Friendships represent "investments of the self" (Hess, 1972:390). The point in the life course at which friendships are established and the periods during which they are maintained therefore reveal self-conception in a biographical context. The independent informants had rarely known their associates for long periods of time. If they did, it was not because of their own initiative but due to happenstance. Support for selves present in earlier periods in their lives was absent. For them, there were no others except in some cases spouses and kin who had "known them when. . . . " Although newly established relationships were almost always with members of the same age cohort—individuals with whom they were able to share memories of historical events and who may even have shared similar backgrounds (Hochschild, 1978)—these were abstract memories, not shared ones. Memories of former selves were not verifiable in relationships. In Redfoot and Back's words, only "immediate needs and activities" explained current relationships.

For the discerning, because they had maintained relationships with others whom they had known for a long time, significant parts of the self not only were available but, in essence, were preserved in those relationships. The immigrant whose only friendships were with members of the social club to which he had belonged in early adulthood and with two fellow immigrants he had met when he first arrived in the United States is an example of someone for whom biographical significance was all-important. Another example is the man who had maintained a close friendship into old age only with someone who "knew me when I was knee high to a duck." This is quite different from establishing new ties in old age. Except for those who had become independent in early adulthood or for whom deaths had robbed them of their friends, the discerning had only long-term friendships, initially established early in their lives. These friends supported what might be described as a "historical" self—the self that was available in the period of the life course when the friendship was established, was frozen, almost as if the "development of the self" (Breytspraak, 1984) had been halted.

The friendships of the acquisitive informants included, in most cases, both biographical and immediate significance. They described both long-term and relatively short-term relationships, so that aspects of self were both conserved and added. A case in point is the man who had maintained ties from adolescence with members of his Boy Scout troop but who had continued to add friends throughout his life as circumstances changed. Another is the woman who had distinct periods in her life—childhood, early marriage, childrearing, widowhood, job, and move to retirement community—from each of which friends were drawn. For them, friendships represented their biographies. Friendship style, then, indicates the degree to which the self is conceived in biographic context or only housed in the present.

C.P. Snow (1960:268) wrote of the significance of old friends to the support of the "historical" self when he described the meeting of two old friends:

> And yet, though the physical transformation was dramatic, though time had done its trick, and she sat there, a middle-aged woman filling her chair—I did not quite, at least, not with photographic acceptance, see her so. I did not see her as I should have seen her if I had that night come into her house for the first time, and been confronted with her—as I had been confronted with those great matriarchs of aunts, having no pictures of their past. Somehow anyone whom one has known from youth one never sees quite straight: the picture has been doubly exposed; something of themselves when young, the physical presence of themselves when young, lingers till they die.

The independent informants and the acquisitive who did not maintain long-term relationships had ties only with those who saw them with "photographic acceptance," while for those who had ties with friends procured in earlier periods of their lives, not only the self of the moment but the history of the self was available as well.

From the social-psychological perspective, then, these friendship styles can be viewed as strategies for supporting an individual's self-conception, not only in the present, but within a biographical context as well. The styles, of course, are not completely within the control of the individual. Most immediately, a friendship bond depends on the actions of two people, so that a decision by one to end the relationship relegates the bond only to the past. Moreover, social location and changes in circumstance that are not in an individual's purview are important as well. Leopold Rosenmayr (1982:32) describes the cumulative significance of social class membership:

> The internalization of socioeconomic disadvantages and the gradual acceptance of low standards depresses expectations even further and reduces or extinguishes aspirations. The individual, as the last part of this chain of causation, becomes instrumental in his or her own handicap, so that we may speak of "self-induced *social* deprivation" [p. 32].

> In the course of the lifelong socialization processes, class-specific attitudes are developed that may be substantial impediments to planned and rational behavior from which the individual might have benefited, or might still benefit, given different social encouragement and support [p. 46].

There can be no doubt that the social stratification of life chances affects choices made by individuals about the value both of self and of long-term relationships. With respect specifically to social class, however, in each of the three categories of friendship style, persons from all social classes were represented. This stems in part from the fact that half of the informants were women, some of whom had never been married, and identifying the social class of women is problematic. In part it also is because the availability of temporal information about factors used to gauge socioeconomic status, rather than data reflecting only one point in time, makes the assignment of social class less clear-cut.

Informants were both upwardly and downwardly mobile throughout their lives. Some might have been classified misleadingly as lower class on the basis of their occupations: An office cleaner, for example, enjoyed leisure pursuits (e.g., opera and ballet) usually considered the purview of members of higher classes. In addition, gender was not related to friendship style. Herbert Blumer (1956) chastized sociologists for depending on "variable analysis" in research. The use of biographical data, in contrast to responses at one point in time to questions about education and occupation, supports his contention that it is easy to lose sight of what the variable represents in the real world.

It would be unwarranted to assume that the friendship styles exhibited by people in old age accurately characterizes them throughout life. The informants presented their biographies consistently, as if the roots of their adopting the style lay in childhood. However, there is a very real possibility that their styles changed through the life course and that informants "rewrote" their biographies to match changed expectations. Agnes Hankiss (1981:204) writes:

> The adult person's life-model is probably the result of numerous "mutations," key events, either personal or historic in nature, which constantly lead or force that person to select new models, a new strategy of life. This instrumental role played by the process of transposing reality into mythology is linked to this particular need for adaptation, to this symbiotic relationship between the *old* and the *new* [emphasis in original].

It cannot be ignored that the styles identified here are drawn from oral biographies of persons near the ends of their lives who indeed have undergone "numerous mutations." Collecting oral biographies from younger persons would shed light on the possibility that the styles are not the result of psychological proclivities established early in life but are strategies that develop in response to events experienced during the life course.

The Life-Course Perspective and Friendship

In evaluating the findings presented here from the life-course perspective, the goal was to discover the relationship between friendships and "turnings," or transitions, in individuals' lives. David Mandelbaum (1973:181) writes: "A turning is accomplished when the person takes on a new set of roles, enters into fresh relations with a new set of people and acquires a new self-conception." Social scientists who have written about friendship through the life cycle (see, e.g., Bensman and Lilienfeld, 1979; Brown, 1981; Dickens and Perlman, 1981; Lowenthal et al., 1975) divide the life span into stages in which individuals require different things from friends for reasons that conform to the particular theoretical perspective being explicated. B. Bradford Brown (1981:43), for example, identifies six stages—infancy, childhood, adolescence, young adulthood, middle adulthood, and old age—in each of which "the focal concern of friendship seems to shift. . . . As the needs or 'developmental tasks' confronting an individual shift across age, so do the primary functions friends serve."

Beth Hess (1972:36), on the other hand, approaches the issue of change through the life course somewhat differently:

> The number and type of friendships open to an individual at particular stages of his life course depend less upon explicit age criteria for the friendship role itself than upon the *other* roles that he plays. As his total cluster of roles changes over his lifetime, so do his friendship relations undergo change [emphasis in original].

Her conceptualization allows an examination not only of the external forces imposed by development and norms but of the actual role changes that constitute a particular biography. Chronological age is often used as the institutionalized criterion for the timing of transitions (e.g., school-leaving and retirement). The significant transitions in individuals' lives, however, are both personal and normative (Neugarten and Hagestad, 1976). In times of rapid social change—which clearly characterizes the century in which these informants' lives were unfolding—personally significant transitions are likely to take precedence over normative ones (Zurcher, 1977).

The transitions related to friendships that stand out in these oral biographies were moves, changes in jobs, and changes in marital status. In some cases these occurred "on time," but in others they were "off time" (Neugarten and Hagestad, 1976). Regardless of timing for the independent and acquisitive informants, they were often significant with respect to friendships. Transitions were used implicitly and sometimes explicitly as explanations for both the "fading away" and the initiation of friendships. They provided individuals with the opportunity to meet new people who might be befriended. However, for the discerning and many of the acquisitive, continuity in friendship ties also was clear. In conjunction with examining "continuities and discontinuities of role and setting over the course of life," Sally Falk Moore (1978:24) recommends looking at continuity in social relations throughout the life course as well:

> Both continuities/discontinuities, and cumulation of various kinds may take place in an individual's *social relations*, and this may well be the most important element of all, both analytically and experientially.... Social relationships may be accumulated over time, and at one point or another they may be lost and broken off. They may become more intense—i.e., the cumulation over time may be in the intensifying and strengthening of the relationship in terms of emotional investment, common experience, long-term exchanges. Thus, cumulation may be of numbers of relationships, or of kind and quality of relationships, or both. But social ties may be destroyed as well as built. They may be lost through disputes, death, emigration, and the like. In each society the continuities/discontinuities and the cumulations/losses are different in content, in significant events, in style [emphasis in original].

It is difficult to characterize a society as complex and pluralistic as the United States. Rather, what the informants' topical oral biographies reveal is the variety of patterns with respect to continuity and cumulations through the life course. What is clear for the discerning and most of the acquisitive is that transitions do not mark discontinuities in friendships. For the discerning, once friendships were established, transitions were not perceived as relevant. For the acquisitive, transitions were important with respect to cumulation, but not with respect to continuity. They expected to maintain the old while adding new friendships.

Another goal of the life-course perspective is to discover the effects of historical events or periods on the subsequent trajectories of those who are affected by them, especially at ages in the life cycle when significant decisions are made, such as whether to continue education or to have children (Elder, 1974). Tamara Hareven (1982:1) writes: "Underlying a life course approach is the assumption that . . . the position that people experience in later years of life is molded by the cumulative life history and by *the specific historical conditions affecting their lives at earlier times*" [emphasis in original]. These informants lived through important and wrenching historical periods including, for some, World War I, and, for all, the Depression and World War II. Perhaps if the number of people included in this project were larger, patterns would have emerged. However, the variety of ways in which the informants referred to the effects on their friendships of the historical periods through which they lived defied arriving at definitive statements.

For a few, history apparently affected not only with whom they established friendships but also the style of friendship they adopted. An example is the immigrant, the discerning informant cited above, who enjoyed relatively high status in his youth which he did not achieve in the United States. For him, the cumulation of social relations as well as status and power stopped early in his life. One can at least speculate about whether this is the explanation for his adopting a discerning style of friendship. For most, not style, but the particular friends that they claimed were affected by history. A case in point is the discerning informant who had two very good friends with whom he had maintained ties into middle age. He had established ties with them when he worked as an office boy immediately after high school in the early 1930s. Both of his friends had college degrees but, because of the Depression, were unable to continue their education or to find other work. The informant's opportunity to befriend these particular men, who belonged to a higher social class than he, was made possible by the Depression. The decision for those who graduated from high school during the Depression not to go, to postpone going, or to choose the least expensive way to go to college was offered by a number of people as a reason that high school friendships were either terminated or continued. The ethnic neighborhoods in which a number of the informants had grown up were a product of the wave of immigration, primarily from Eastern Europe, in the early part of the century. Having grown up in one of these ethnic enclaves continued to affect people's social ties throughout their lives. One informant postponed her marriage because of the Depression ("We couldn't marry because I couldn't get a job and he couldn't get a job"), and this may have strengthened her relationship with her college friend: "So I went to New York where my [college] friend said she could put me on [a job] for four dollars a day and that was very good, so I had two or three years in New York City."

Thus, it is clear from the interviews that the particular friendships described by the informants were affected by the historical periods in which they lived, periods that brought specific people together to make possible the establishment of ties. Not as clear, however, is what effect this had on specific friendships or on friendship style. The fact that the woman's "college friend" was able to find a job for her in New York City may or may not have had an effect on their friendship. The immigrant who belonged to the social club in his early adult years might have been discerning regardless of the interference of World War II, although in all likelihood adopting the style would have had very different consequences. However, informants who experienced disasters comparable to his did not stop accumulating friendship ties.

Two of the "presuppositions" that Gregory Bateson (1979) thought "every schoolboy knows . . . " or, more accurately, *should* know are relevant to this impasse. The first is that "divergent sequences are unpredictable":

> The generic we can know, but the specific eludes us [p. 45]. . . . There is a deep gulf between statements about an identified individual and statements about a class. Such statements are of *different logical type*, and prediction from one to the other is always unsure. The statement "The liquid is boiling" is of a different logical type from "That molecule will be the first to go" [pp. 45-46, emphasis in original].

Individuals undergo transitions throughout their lives—some normative, some related to the historical period in which they live, and some based more clearly on personal decisions. Predicting what effect these will have on a particular individual's friendships, however, is not possible. The second presupposition, "causality does not work backward," refers to the lure of the "teleological fallacy":

> The Greeks were inclined to believe in what were later called *final* causes. They believed that the pattern generated at the end of a sequence of events could be regarded as in some way causal of the pathway followed by that sequence [p. 66, emphasis in original].

It would be easy to look for "final causes" that would portend a particular informant's being independent, discerning, or acquisitive. Certainly there are explanations that "make sense." For the immigrant cited above, for example, World War II apparently caused a painful discontinuity in his life. The temptation is to attribute his being categorized as discerning to this experience. Other informants, however, experienced similar tragedies and continued to acquire friends, to trust people. From the life-course perspective, then, moving from the individual life to generic statements about friendship is difficult because of the nature of the particular social relationship that is under examination here. This is the subject of the following section.

The Cultural Meaning of Friendship

Two scholars' views of culture were cited in the first chapter. One was David Mandelbaum (1973: 180), who writes: "The cultural dimension has to do with expectations and known forms shared by the people of a group, with the cognitive and normative thought they have in common." The other was Glen Elder (1978:23), who describes "institutionalized specifications" that "constitute a framework of social rules, standards of evaluation, and expectations that link behavior to rewards and negative sanctions." In analyzing the oral biographies using the cultural perspective, then, the goal was to discover patterns—definitions and expectations that the informants held in common. To some degree this has been accomplished in the analysis presented above. With respect especially to cross-gender friendships, the existence of clear expectations to which almost all the informants subscribed were discovered. In other cases— for example, the three different relationships between marriage and friendship—not one, but a number of patterns emerged. The three styles of friendship are another case in point. However, relatively few definitive statements can be made. Lillian Rubin (1981:106) speaks for many sociologists who have focused on friendships when she writes: "[It] is a slippery subject at best—without institutional form, without a clearly defined set of norms for behavior or an agreed-upon set of reciprocal rights and obligations, without even any widely shared agreement about what is a friend." The material reported above supports her contention. There is a great deal of evidence to indicate that the "culture of friendship" is too diverse to capture with a clearly specified set of norms and expectations.

The difficulty of identifying cultural dimensions was acknowledged in the first chapter when it was argued that friendship has somewhat different features from other social relationships. Drawing on Georg Simmel's theoretical discussion of group size, it was argued that because friendship is the ideal typical dyadic relationship based entirely on the individualities of its two members, it is sociologically trivial. To accentuate this point the criteria essential for institutionalization outlined by Peter Berger and Thomas Luckmann (1967) were also applied to friendship to show that two of the essential five are absent and the others somewhat weakly represented. Further evidence is found in the insightful analysis by Robert Paine (1969) who, grappling with the difficulty of defining friendship, described it in contradictory fashion as an "institutionalized non-institution." From a cultural perspective, then, the problem with which sociologists must contend is the somewhat paradoxical evidence that there are very few clear cultural dimensions even though the word "friend" is part of everyone's vocabulary and is used in everyday conversation with faith that meaning is shared.

This situation presents problems for research. More significantly, however, it presents problems for sociological theory. To speak of institutionalization is to speak of roles. Talcott Parsons and Edward Shils (1951:191), for example, wrote that institutionalization means "the integration of the complementary role expectation and sanction patterns with a generalized value system *common* to the members of the more inclusive collectively, of which the system of complementary role-actions may be a part" [emphasis in original]. Or, as Stephen Mennell interprets (1974:75), "In plainer English, the role of shop assistant is highly institutionalized because everyone knows and accepts the usual patterns of action which constitute the minimum characteristics of the role. Therefore, the assistant and all her [sic] customers can judge whether she is adequately and consistently playing the role." Similarly, Berger and Luckmann (1967:74) write:

> The construction of role typologies is a necessary correlate of the institutionalization of conduct. . . . In the common stock of knowledge there are standards of role performance that are accessible to all members of a society, at least to those who are potential performers of the roles in question. This general accessibility is itself part of the same stock of knowledge; not only are the standards of role X generally known, but it is known *that* these standards are known. Consequently every putative actor of role X can be held responsible for abiding by the standards, which can be taught as part of the institutional tradition and used to verify the credentials of all performers and, by the same token, serve as controls [emphasis in original].

It is clear from the evidence presented above, however, that there is no one who can judge objectively whether someone is "adequately and consistently playing the role" of friend. Neither can "every putative actor" who is behaving as a friend be "held responsible for abiding by the standards." Standards apparently are not taught consistently but, for the most part, are negotiated between members of a friendship dyad, each of whom even may evaluate their relationship differently.

Scholars who follow George Herbert Mead and use a symbolic interactionist perspective also have used role in their theoretical writings but have attempted to give role occupants more flexibility—less prescription and more individual initiative:

> Ralph Turner speaks of . . . *external validation* of a role. This happens when: "the behaviour is judged to constitute a role by others whose judgements are felt to have some claim to correctness or legitimacy. The simplest form of such a criterion is discovery of a name in common use for the role. If the pattern of behaviour can be readily assigned a name, it acquires *ipso facto* the exteriority and constraint of Durkheim's 'collective representations'" (1962:30). But, with greater caution than Linton or Parsons and Shils, Turner immediately adds that "Naming does not assure [sic] that there will be agreement on the content of the role; it merely insures that people will do their disagreeing as if there were something real about which to disagree" [Mennell, 1974:75].

The informants clearly felt that norms and expectations existed for friendships. This was most obvious in their unwillingness to refer to personal experience as theirs alone. Very few people used "I" or "my" to describe their experiences. Instead almost all used the normative "you" as if they were citing rules that everyone recognized. Most people generalized from their own personal experiences. One example among many is a woman who said, "As a widow you walk a much more careful line in how you do things than when you were married. Life is much prettier and easier when you're a married couple." Clearly, this is her own experience, but rather than seeing it as only one possibility, she projects it to all widows. In only a few cases did informants say, in essence, "this is my experience, but I'm not sure about anyone else." Instead they saw their experiences as "typical." There was a "name in common use," then, and belief that there was a "pattern of behavior;" but, in fact, there was not a great deal of agreement. If naming does not ensure agreement, what sociological insight is added by describing friend as a role? How can there be a noninstitutionalized role? Simply because people can use a word without hesitation, assuming that meaning is shared, does not mean that a role in fact exists.

One way that symbolic interactionists have attempted to circumvent the reification implicit in the concept of role is to add the concept of identity. Thomas Scheff (1973:204), for example, defines identity as "the pattern of behavior that is mutually recognized as characterizing one of the participants in a transaction by those participants." He distinguishes identity from role:

> Role is a concept, like identity, that refers to the individual contribution to a transaction. I take role to be the narrrower of the two, however. Role is part of the social structure, i.e., part of the generally recognized pattern of expectations in a community. Situational identity, on the other hand, is tied to a particular person in a particular situation. An individual's situational identity may well be his social role; it need not necessarily be, however [p. 204].

Thus identity, because it is situational, makes sense only within the context of interaction. In institutionalized relationships, both role and identity are present. A wife, for example, recognizes a man as her husband, his role, but also *evaluates* him as *her* husband, his identity. For noninstitutionalized relationships, role is absent and only the evaluation or assignment of identity is available. As Graham Allan (1979:34) points out, for friendship "it is the actual relationship itself that is the most important factor in deciding whether someone can or cannot be labelled a friend." Using only the concept of identity to explain friendships, however, "leads implicitly to the supposition that an ideographic, and purely descriptive, social science is possible" (Mennell, 1974:60). Using only the concept of identity to explicate the friend relationship omits too much. In summary, to speak of the role of friend is a contradiction, because friend does not denote "an expected sequence of behavior"(Scheff, 1973:204). To use only identity, however, is also inadequate, because the only general statement that can be made is that friendships are negotiated between two individuals. What is missing is a sociological concept that focuses on relationships.

Friendship is by definition an egalitarian relationship. This does not mean that two friends have equal status but that, regardless of the status each enjoys outside the relationship, in it they are equal by definition. Gerald Suttles (1970:97) writes:

> The generalized character of friendship creates a note of equality, which enjoins those in the same or different institutions to moderate their differences; friendship, then, has a leveling influence not only among friends but among all others drawn together within the same congregation. The friends of friends are required to treat each other as equals.

Egalitarian relationships may be more common than is acknowledged, but they are rarely studied by sociologists. John Lofland (1976:113) argues that this is because they are rare. An alternate explanation is that they do not fit into the available conceptual schemes. The difficulty of predicting—finding patterns—in dyadic egalitarian relationships is addressed by Norbert Elias (1978). He uses "game models" as a heuristic device to demonstrate the "processual character of relationships between interdependent people." In a two-person game, such as tug of war, when two players have equal strength neither can control the process of the game because "the course of the game . . . passes beyond the control of either" (Mennell, 1974:83-84).

> Predicting the state of even a two person game like chess, say twelve moves ahead, is extremely difficult. There are numerous possible outcomes with differing degrees of likelihood. What is more, the probabilities change with each successive move [Mennell, 1974:84].

Predicting the course of egalitarian relationships, then, is impossible, not only for the social scientist, but for the participants as well. There can be no rules to fall back on, except those negotiated by the two individuals, and no guarantee that the other will respond in a predictable way. The two women whose friends responded differently when they became blind illustrate this well, for in both cases there was a clear test to the assumption that the relationship was predictable. In one the assumption was justified, in the other, not. Relationships that had existed for a long time are another case in point. Even when they were no longer "satisfactory," they often were maintained. The lengthy history of the friendship committed its members to act in accord with one another's expectations.

The study of friendship, then, confronts the sociologist with a critical test to theoretical formulations, not only about friendships but about the social organization of societies more generally. Noninstitutionalized relationships, of which friendship is a prime example, either have been relegated to the field of psychology or forced to fit into the available theoretical frameworks and described as if they were institutionalized. Reformulating sociological theory so that it can embrace this social relationship would seem to be more fruitful. If the theoretical perspectives do not fit, perhaps they are inadequate. If the concept of role does not apply to friendship, does this mean that friendships are irrelevant or that role theories are limited? Norbert Elias (1978:75) suggests the latter: "Sociological theories which make it appear that norms are the mainspring of social relationships cannot account for the possibility of human relationships without norms and regulations; they give a distorted view of human societies." For the sociologist, then, theory may be advanced by attempts to bring friendship into the fold.

APPENDIX: INTERVIEW GUIDE

Looking back over your life and including the present, who are the persons you consider to be friends?

(1) *Listen and probe as person talks. Encourage informant to relate life history with friends as the thread.*

(2) *Ask specific questions about each friend as needed.*

Specific information about each friend mentioned:

How old were you?

Where were you living?

How did you meet this person?

How old was this person?

Do you remember what happened in particular that made you think of this person as a friend rather than as an acquaintance?

Why did you consider this person your friend (attributes, activities, etc.)?

What (do/did) you do with this friend?

Do you still consider this person to be a friend? Why or why not?

When did you last have contact with this person?

Have your feelings about this person changed through the years?

Did you ever feel that you couldn't do something for this person that she or he wanted you to do? vice versa? (conflict between friends, friends and spouse/family)

Were you friends with this person at the same time you were friends with another person?

Cross-Gender Friendships:

Have you ever been friends with someone of the other gender?

How is/was this different from being friends with someone of the same gender? *or*

Why do you think you have never had a friend who was male/female?

Ex-friends:

Is there anyone who was a friend of yours at one time who is no longer a friend? What happened? (active/passive split)

General questions about friendships:

Ideally speaking, what is a friend? What is your definition of friendship with someone?

Why do you think you have maintained friendships with some people and not with others?

Thinking back over all your friends, who is or was your best friend? Why was/is this person special? (Comparisons among friends mentioned)

Do you consider your spouse or other relatives to be friends, or do you think of friends and relatives differently?

Do (or did) you share friends with your spouse or do (did) you each have friends?

If you were asked to give advice to someone about how to make a friend, what would your advice be?

Who was the *last* friend that you made? (Have you made any friends in the last few years?) Do you think of your new friends differently from the friends you made earlier in your life?

Have there been times when you had to choose between two friends? Between your spouse or family and a friend?

Have there been periods in your life when you felt that you had no friends? When friends mattered more than other times?

Demographic variables:

Age

Gender

SES history

Educational history

Occupational history

Geographic mobility history

Marital history

Parental history

REFERENCES

Allan, Graham A. (1979) A Sociology of Friendship and Kinship. Boston: George Allen and Unwin.

Altman, Irwin and Dalmas A. Taylor (1973) Social Penetration: The Development of Interpersonal Relationships. New York: Holt, Rinehart & Winston.

Arling, Greg (1976) "The elderly widow and her family, neighbors, and friends." Journal of Marriage and the Family 38:757-768.

Babchuk, Nicholas and Alan P. Bates (1963) "The primary relations of middle-class couples: a study in male dominance." American Sociological Review 28:377-384.

Bates, Alan P. and Nicholas Babchuk (1961) "The primary group: a re-appraisal." Sociological Quarterly 2:181-191.

Bateson, Gregory (1979) Mind and Nature: A Necessary Unity. New York: Bantam.

Becker, Howard S. (1970) "The relevance of life histories," pp. 419-428 in Norman K. Denzin (ed.) Sociological Methods: A Sourcebook. Chicago: Aldine.

Bensman, Joseph and Robert Lilienfeld (1979) Between Public and Private: Lost Boundaries of the Self. New York: Free Press.

Berger, Peter L. (1963) Invitation to Sociology: A Humanistic Perspective. Garden City, NY: Anchor.

———and Thomas Luckmann (1967) The Social Construction of Reality. Garden City, NY: Anchor.

Bertaux, Daniel (1981) "Introduction," pp. 5-15 in Daniel Bertaux (ed.) Biography and Society: The Life History Approach in the Social Sciences. Beverly Hills, CA: Sage.

———and Martin Kohli (1984) "The life course approach: a continental view." Annual Review of Sociology 10:215-237.

Blau, Zena Smith (1961) "Structural constraints on friendship in old age." American Sociological Review 26:429-439.

Blumer, Herbert (1956) "Sociological analysis and the 'variable.'" American Sociology Review 21:683-690.

Booth, Alan (1972) "Sex and social participation." American Sociological Review 37:183-192.

———and Elaine Hess (1974) "Cross-sex friendship." Journal of Marriage and the Family 36:38-47.

Bott, Elizabeth (1971) Family and Social Network. New York: Free Press.

Brenton, Myron (1974) Friendship. New York: Stein & Day.

Breytspraak, Linda M. (1984) The Development of Self in Later Life. Boston: Little, Brown.

Brown, B. Bradford (1981) "A life-span approach to friendship: age-related dimensions of an ageless relationship," pp. 23-50 in Helena Lopata and David Maines (eds.) Research on the Interweave of Social Roles, Volume 2: Friendship. Greenwich, CT: JAI Press.

Butler, Robert N. (1963) "The life review: an interpretation of reminiscence in the aged."
    Psychiatry: Journal of the Study of Inter-Personal Processes 26:65-76.
Candy, Sandra Elizabeth G. (1976) "A comparative analysis of friendship functions in six
    groups of men and women." Ph.D. dissertation, Wayne State University.
Crapanzano, Vincent (1977) "The life history in anthropological field work." Anthro-
    pology and Humanism Quarterly, 2:3-7.
Dickens, Wendy J. and Daniel Perlman (1981) "Friendship over the life-cycle," pp. 91-122
    in Steve Duck and Robin Gilmour (eds.) Personal Relationships 2: Developing
    Personal Relationships. New York: Academic Press.
Duck, Steven W. (1973) Personal Relationships and Personal Constructs: A Study of
    Friendship Formation. New York: John Wiley and Sons.
Eisenstadt, S. N. (1956) "Ritualized personal relations." Man 96:90-95.
Elder, Glen H. (1974) Children of the Great Depression. Chicago: University of Chicago
    Press.
———(1978) "Family history and the life course," in Tamara K. Hareven (ed.)
    Transitions: The Family and the Life Course in Historical Perspective. New York:
    Academic Press.
———(ed.) (1984) Life Course Dynamics: Trajectories and Transitions, 1968-1980.
    Ithaca, NY: Cornell University Press.
Elias, Norbert (1978) What is Sociology? New York, NY: Columbia University Press.
Erikson, Erik H. (1959) Identity and the Life Cycle: Psychological Issues. New York:
    International Universities Press.
Fischer, Claude S. (1982) To Dwell Among Friends. Chicago: University of Chicago
    Press.
Fischer, Lucy Rose (1982) "Sociology and life history: methodological incongruence."
    International Journal of Oral History 4:29-40.
Frank, Gelya (1979) "Finding the common denominator: a phenomenological critique of
    life history method." Ethos 7:68-94.
———(1980) "Life histories in gerontology: the subjective side of aging," pp. 155-176 in
    Christine L. Fry and Jennie Keith (eds.) New Methods for Old Age Research: Anthro-
    pological Alternatives. Chicago: Loyola University.
Glick, Paul and Robert Parke (1965) "New approaches to studying the life cycle of the
    family." Demography 2:187-202.
Goffman, Erving (1963) Stigma: Notes on the Management of Spoiled Identity.
    Englewood Cliffs, NJ: Prentice-Hall.
Gold, Herbert (1973) "Friendship and the lifeboat." Harper's Magazine 246:44-47.
Granovetter, Mark S. (1973) "The strength of weak ties." American Journal of Sociology
    78:1360-1380.
Greenwald, Anthony G. (1980) "The totalitarian ego: fabrication and revision of personal
    history." American Psychologist 35:603-618.
Hankiss, Agnes (1981) "Ontologies of the self: on the mythological rearranging of one's
    life history," pp. 203-209 in Daniel Bertaux (ed.) Biography and Society: The Life
    History Approach in the Social Sciences. Beverly Hills, CA: Sage.
Hareven, Tamara K. (1981) "Historical changes in the timing of family traditions," pp.
    143-165 in Robert W. Fogel et al. (eds.) Aging: Stability and Change in the Family.
    New York: Academic Press.
———(1982) "The life course in historical perspective," pp. 1-26 in Tamara K. Hareven
    and Kathleen J. Adams (eds.) Aging and Life Course Transitions: An Interdisciplinary
    Perspective. New York: Guilford Press.

Hess, Beth (1972) "Friendship," pp. 357-393 in Matilda White Riley et al. (eds.) Aging and Society, Volume 3: A Sociology of Age Stratification. New York: Russell Sage Foundation.

Heyl, Barbara S. (1979) The Madam as Entrepreneur: Career Management in House Prostitution. New Brunswick, NJ: Transaction.

Hindley, C. B. (1979) "Problems in interviewing: obtaining retrospective information," pp. 100-114 in Louis Moss and Harvey Goldstein (eds.) The Recall Method in Social Surveys. London: University of London Institute of Education.

Hochschild, Arlie Russell (1978) The Unexpected Community. Berkeley, CA: University of California Press.

Huston, Ted L. and George Levinger (1978) "Interpersonal attraction and relationships." Annual Review of Psychology 29:115-156.

Jerrome, Dorothy (1981) "The significance of friendship for women in later life," Ageing and Society 1:175-197.

Kessler, Suzanne J. and Wendy McKenna (1978) Gender: An Ethnomethodological Approach. New York: Wiley.

Kurth, Suzanne B. (1970) "Friendships and friendly relations," pp. 136-170 in George J. McCall (ed.), Social Relationships. Chicago: Aldine.

Langness, L. L. (1965) The Life History in Anthropological Science. New York: Holt, Rinehart & Winston.

———and Gelya Frank (1981) Lives: An Anthropological Approach to Biography. Novato, CA: Chandler & Sharp.

Laumann, Edward O. (1966) Prestige and Association in an Urban Community. New York: Bobbs-Merrill.

———(1969) "Friends of urban men: an assessment of accuracy in reporting their socio-economic attributes, mutual choice and attitude agreement." Sociometry 32: 54-69.

Lazarsfeld, Paul F. and Robert K. Merton (1954) "Friendship as social process: a substantive and methodological analysis," pp. 18-66 in Morroe Berger et al. (eds.) Freedom and Control in Modern Society. New York: Van Nostrand.

Levinger, George and Harold L. Raush (eds.) (1977) Close Relationships: Perspectives on the Meaning of Intimacy. Amherst, MA: University of Massachusetts Press.

Lofland, John (1971) Analyzing Social Settings: A Guide to Qualitative Observations and Analysis. Belmont, CA: Wadsworth.

———(1976) Doing Social Life. New York: John Wiley.

———and Lyn H. Lofland (1984) Analyzing Social Settings: A Guide to Qualitative Analysis. Belmont, CA: Wadsworth.

Lowenthal, Marjorie Fiske and Clayton Haven (1968) "Interaction and adaptations: intimacy as a critical variable," pp. 390-400 in Bernice L. Neugarten (ed.) Middle Age and Aging. Chicago: University of Chicago Press.

———and Betsy Robinson (1976) "Social networks and isolation," pp. 432-456 in Robert H. Binstock and Ethel Shanas (eds.) Handbook of Aging and the Social Sciences. New York: Van Nostrand.

———Majda Thurnher, David Chiriboga, and Associates (1975) Four Stages of Life: A Comprehensive Study of Women and Men Facing Transitions. San Francisco, CA: Jossey-Bass.

Mandelbaum, David B. (1973) "The study of life history: Gandhi." Current Anthropology 14:177-196.

Marshall, Victor W. (1980) Last Chapters: A Sociology of Aging and Dying. Monterey, CA: Brooks/Cole.

Matthews, Sarah H. (1979) The Social World of Old Women: Management of Self-Identity. Beverly Hills, CA: Sage.

————(1983) "Definitions of friendship and their consequences in old age." Ageing and Society 3:141-155.

McCall, George J. (1970) "The social organization of relationships," pp. 3-34 in George J. McCall (ed.) Social Relationships. Chicago: Aldine.

Mennell, Stephen (1974) Sociological Theory: Uses and Unities. New York, NY: Praeger.

Moore, Sally Falk (1978) "Old age in a life-term social arena: some Chagga of Kilimanjaro in 1974," pp. 23-75 in Barbara G. Myerhoff and Andrei Simic (eds.) Life's Career-Aging: Cultural Variations on Growing Old. Beverly Hills, CA: Sage.

Munnichs, Joep M. A. (1964) "Loneliness, isolation, and social relations in old age: a pilot survey." Vita Humana 7:228-238.

Myerhoff, Barbara (1979) Number Our Days. New York: E. P. Dutton.

————and Andrei Simic (1978) Life's Career—Aging: Cultural Variations on Growing Old. Beverly Hills, CA: Sage.

Neugarten, Bernice L. and Gunhild O. Hagestad (1976) "Age and the life course," pp. 35-55 in Robert H. Binstock and Ethel Shanas (eds.) Handbook of Aging and the Social Sciences. New York: Van Nostrand Reinhold.

————Joan W. Moore, and John C. Lowe (1968) "Age norms, age constraints, and adult socialization," pp. 22-28 in Bernice L. Neugarten (ed.) Middle Age and Aging. Chicago: University of Chicago Press.

Nydegger, Corinne N. (1981) "On being caught up in time." Human Development 24:1-23.

Paine, Robert (1969) "In search of friendship: an exploratory analysis in 'middle-class' culture." Man 4:505-524.

Parsons, Talcott and Edward A. Shils (eds.) (1951) Toward a General Theory of Action. Cambridge, MA: Harvard University Press.

Phillips, Derek L. (1969) "Social class, social participation and happiness: a consideration of interaction opportunities and investment." Sociological Quarterly 10:3-21.

Pitt-Rivers, Julian (1968) "Pseudo-Kinship," International Encyclopedia of the Social Sciences. New York: Macmillan.

Powers, Edward A. and Gordon L. Bultena (1976) "Sex differences in intimate friendships of old age." Journal of Marriage and the Family 38:739-747.

Pritchitt, Victor S. (1977) Autobiography. London: The English Association.

Redfoot, Donald and Kurt Back (1984) "The perceptual presence of the life course." Presented at the annual meeting of the Gerontological Society of America, San Antonio, TX.

Reina, Ruben E. (1959) "Two patterns of friendship in a Guatemalan community." American Anthropologist 61:44-50.

Reisman, John J. (1979) Anatomy of Friendship. New York: Irvington.

Riley, Matilda White (1976) "Age strata in social systems," pp. 189-217 in Robert H. Binstock and Ethel Shanas (eds.) Handbook of Aging and the Social Sciences. New York: Van Nostrand.

————(1985) "Women, men, and the lengthening life course," pp. 333-347 in Alice S. Rossi (ed.) Gender and the Life Course. New York: Aldine.

————and Anne Foner (1968) "Friends and neighbors," pp. 561-575 in Matilda White Riley and Anne Foner (eds.) Aging and Society, Vol. 1: An Inventory of Research Findings. New York: Russell Sage Foundation.

————Marilyn Johnson, and Anne Foner (1972) Aging and Society, Vol. 3: A Sociology of Age Stratification. New York: Russell Sage Foundation.

Rosengarten, Theodore (1979) "Stepping over cockleburs: conversations with Ned Cobb," pp. 104-131 in M. Pachter (ed.) Telling Lives. Washington, DC: New Republic Books/National Portrait Gallery.

Rosenmayr, Leopold (1981) "Objective and subjective perspectives of life span research." Ageing and Society 1:29-49.

———(1982) "Biography and identity," pp. 27-53 in Tamara K. Hareven and Kathleen J. Adams (eds.) Aging and Life Course Transitions: An Interdisciplinary Perspective. New York: Guilford Press.

Rosow, Irving (1967) Social Integration of the Aged. New York: The Free Press.

Ross, Jennie-Keith (1977) Old People, New Lives: Community Creation in a Retirement Residence. Chicago: University of Chicago Press.

Rubin, Lillian B. (1981) "Sociological research: the subjective dimension: the 1980 SSSI distinguished lecture." Symbolic Interaction 4:97-112.

Scheff, Thomas J. (1973) "On the concepts of identity and social relationship," pp. 193-207 in Tomatsu Shibutani (ed.) Human Nature and Collective Behavior: Papers in Honor of Herbert Blumer. New Brunswick, NJ: Transaction Books.

Selman, Robert L. (1981) "The child as friendship philosopher," pp. 242-272 in Steven B. Asher and John M. Gottman (eds.) The Development of Children's Friendships. New York: Cambridge University Press.

Shaw, Clifford R. (1930) The Jack Roller. Chicago: University of Chicago Press.

Shulman, Norman (1975) "Life-cycle variations in patterns of close relationships." Journal of Marriage and the Family 37:813-821.

Simic, Andrei and Barbara Myerhoff (1978) "Conclusion," pp. 231-246 in Barbara Myerhoff and Andrei Simic (eds.) Life's Career—Aging: Cultural Variations on Growing Old. Beverly Hills, CA: Sage.

Simmel, Georg (1950) "The isolated individual and the dyad," pp. 118-144 in Kurt H. Wolff (ed.) The Sociology of Georg Simmel. New York: The Free Press.

Skolnick, Arlene (1983) "Looking at lives, or 'whose life course is it, anyway?'" Contemporary Sociology 12:386-387.

Snow, C. P. (1960) The Affair. New York: Charles Scribner's Sons.

Spradley, James P. (1979) The Ethnographic Interview. New York: Holt, Rinehart & Winston.

Strauss, Anselm (1959) Mirrors and Masks: The Search for Identity. Glencoe, IL: The Free Press.

Suttles, Gerald D. (1970) "Friendship as a social institution," pp. 95-135 in George J. McCall (ed.) Social Relationships. Chicago: Aldine.

Townsend, Peter (1957) The Family Life of Old People. London: Routledge & Kegan Paul.

Tremblay, Marc-Alelard (1957) "The key informant technique: a non-ethnographic application." American Anthropologist 59:688-701.

Turner, Ralph H. (1962) "Role-taking: process versus conformity," pp. 20-40 in Arnold M. Rose (ed.) Human Behavior and Social Processes. Boston: Houghton Mifflin.

Verbrugge, Lois M. (1977) "The structure of adult friendship choices." Social Forces 56:576-597.

Weber, Max (1978) Economy and Society: An Outline of Interpretive Sociology. Guenther Roth and Claus Wittich (eds.) Berkeley, CA: University of California Press.

Zurcher, Louis A. (1977) The Mutable Self: A Self-Concept for Social Change. Beverly Hills, CA: Sage.

INDEX

ABOUT THE AUTHOR

Sarah H. Matthews is Associate Professor of Sociology at Case Western Reserve University, where she is Director of the Gerontological Studies Program. She earned her Ph.D. in Sociology from the University of California at Davis. In addition to friendship and biography, she is interested in older families and intergenerational relations and has published in these areas in professional journals. An earlier book, *The Social World of Old Women: Management of Self-Identity*, was also published by Sage Publications.